CHA CHING

There is No Money in
Sales for 2nd Place

MERYL SNOW

Printed in the United States of America

First Printing, 2017

ISBN-13: 978-1542833660
ISBN-10: 1542833663

It's time to pay it forward

Table of Contents

INTRODUCTION 1

CHAPTER 1   How to Hire a 1 in a Million Salesperson 2

CHAPTER 2   Salesperson Contract/Agreement 25

CHAPTER 3   Compensation 36

CHAPTER 4   Training A Salesperson.........................39

CHAPTER 5   Coaching & Mentoring A Salesperson ..47

CHAPTER 6   Setting And Tracking Sales Goals..........56

CHAPTER 7   You Don't Need A Laser Show To Run An
Effective Sales Meeting 65

CHAPTER 8   Employee Evaluation 77
    PART 1 78
    PART 2 78

CHAPTER 9   5 Sales Techniques...............................79

CHAPTER 10   You Said It Without Saying It.............92

CHAPTER 11   And The Survey Says…. 99

CHAPTER 12   Turning Order Takers into Salespeople
....110

CHAPTER 13   Leveraging Social Media 116

CHAPTER 14   Guerilla Marketing............................121

CHAPTER 15   Master Networking by Helping Others
Thrive..126

CHAPTER 16   Preventing your business from being
seen as a commodity – what can you do?..............133

CHAPTER 17 The Vitamin or Painkiller Strategy....139

CHAPTER 18 Why are my competitors Busier? 146

CHAPTER 19 Exercises...149

CHAPTER 20 Now What?.......................................153

INTRODUCTION

There are so many ways by which a company can lose money in business; one of the surest means of losing money is to get the wrong person to do the right job! It is no longer news that the increasing number of employees outweighs the available employment, which does not make it easy for an employer to pick the right person for the job. That is why it became paramount for business owners to have a guardian angel; a piece that will always guide you to get the right person for the job, and that is what CHA CHING promises to do.

CHA CHING has been written for the special events industry with so many practical experiences that make it impossible for the concepts in this book to fail. Much more to that, breaks through the employee's wall of pretence to bring you a genuine, dedicated and capable individual. With the system adopted in CHA CHING; it is practically impossible to hire the wrong person.

Over the years, the system taught in CHA CHING has not only proven to help in picking the right person for the right job; it has also contributed to increasing sales dramatically by bringing out the sales power in every individual. This book contains sales strategies that will add revenue immediately.

CHA CHING was written for all level of business owner and sales people – irrespective of your knowledge; whether you are new or seasoned in the business, CHA CHING always has something for you.

CHAPTER 1

How to Hire a 1 in a Million Salesperson

One of the most common questions I get from my clients is, "how do you hire excellent salespeople?"

This, as you may know, can be easier said than done! Traditional recruitment and interview methods can work well in some cases, but we have all hired an individual this way and been utterly disappointed by the results. While there is no surefire way to ensure that your newly hired salesperson is going to be a winner, I have developed a series of recruiting techniques that have helped me immensely over the years.

But first…

Meet 'Brenda.' She has an English accent Americans love. We connected right away, so much so that I didn't even check her references. I had a good feeling about her, and I hired her immediately, even though she didn't have any experience in special events. She did have marketing and retail experience, and I thought she would be perfect.

Brenda was my first hire. Because of all the horror stories you hear about sales people, I was skeptical at first; however, the following six months proved she did well. She hit all her goals. Then, suddenly, Brenda didn't come to work one day. I felt something was wrong.

MEET BRENDA

I called her several times, but no response. I called again the next day and, still, no Brenda. I only had the information in her new hire packet containing her numbers in London. This was at a time before cell phones, about 27 years ago, so you didn't call overseas. I was apprehensive about her; as this was not like her. Brenda was always on top of everything.

A week went by. We had business to do so I picked up her clients. I called one of them to let them know their deposit was due. The client said she already paid Brenda. In light of this news, I went through all the books, but there weren't any payments listed. I called another client and received the same reply. A third gave the same answer, "I paid Brenda."

Apparently, people wrote checks directly to her. Not only did I waste six months training her but I was now out of a lot of money. The only thing left to do was to call the police. I gave them all the information from her new hire folder. A few days later, they called back to say they didn't know who I had working for me but it wasn't Brenda, the person belonging to the social security number, was in London and they could guarantee that. After more research, it turned out this woman was a fraud, and she stole the identity of her American friend.

The fake Brenda took advantage of my being a young caterer just starting out. I was new to the ways of hiring, checking references and following up on clients. I didn't check my employee's references. Had she given me references though, they probably would have all been good. The real Brenda was doing well in London. Anyway, here's the fake Brenda today.

The impostor was arrested but was not charged for the crimes she committed against my company. She was arrested for other crimes.

I thought I would start out with this story because we all have horror stories of at least one person we've hired. We have businesses, and we put everything into them and the staff, especially our sales people. They're the ones representing our businesses; they're the people on the front lines, so we must be cautious.

Crafting a job ad for results

When I perused ads on different sites, I noticed that companies are confusing job ads with job descriptions. An ad is to sell the applicant. A description is used internally to describe their responsibilities.

Keep the ad short:

- Title that catches applicants' attention
- Intro: Paragraph that summarizes most interesting points of position
- Company Name
- Location
- Qualifications

Who uses Craigslist to find people? Many do. Social media is awesome mainly, because of its sharing feature and because it's free. Friends will share your post. Their friends will share it too. By the end of the day, inquiries have filled your inbox.

Try placing this statement at the bottom of your ad: "Tell us why you are the perfect candidate for this position and leave your phone number for us to call." You will be amazed at how quickly you will weed out applicants that are not qualified.

Here's an ad that targets event chefs, prep cooks, servers, and bartenders. It's really a general ad for the hospitality sector, but still include 'tell us why' at the bottom of the ad. It was surprising who actually answered that question! Again, those who did are the ones that were hired. If they took the time to call and were articulate on the phone, we want them in our team.

For the people who answered the question but have disqualifiers, the retriever evaluates with "I'm not hiring this person, their grammar is off," or whatever the case may be. Just by utilizing this tool, you can weed out a good number of applicants and narrow down the list. You'll end up with the diamonds!

Here's another one. "Join our growing team," is the same kind of ad that includes the catch-phrase "Tell us why you are the perfect candidate." In addition to the ad, the candidate will need to fill out an online application.

You can't spend a ton of time screening applications. When you put an ad in the papers or online, you will get many resumes. Among those who applied, some will only look good on paper; however, this system allows you to hear what they sound like and, specifically, listen to their grammar. We can learn a lot about a person with that one telephone call.

What's impressive about the system? The machine isolates the people who have potential, and those are the job applicants to call back to schedule an interview.

Tip: To ensure memory retention, you'll want to repost the ad weekly.

Surveys

After the applicants pass the phone call test, then send them a survey. This takes place prior to the actual interview to avoid waste of valuable time and money. The survey can be customized to fit the need for more information. With the automated phone call and the survey behind you, you now have better knowledge about the candidate, and you're almost ready to hire.

Here are a few questions to get you started on your survey:

●Describe an important decision you made in the absence of your boss.

●If your friends were asked to describe you, what words would they use?

● What do you feel is your greatest professional accomplishment and failure?

●Give me an example of a goal you achieved and how you reached it.

● What would you do differently if you could start your career over?

● Do you consider yourself successful? Why?

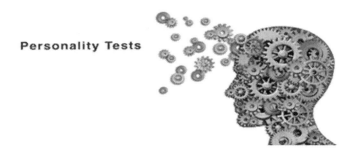

Personality Tests

Personality Tests – Learning about your candidate

As part of our recruitment process, you can ask your candidates to take a short series of standardized personality tests before the first interview. Personality tests will show how to fit new hires into your team. There are many different personality tests available.

For instance,

Caliper Profile

Gallup Strengths

Myers-Briggs

Myers-Briggs seems to be at the top of the list. This test assigns people into 16 different personality types based on their answers to a series of questions. Myers Briggs is easy to understand, and it gives an in-depth analysis.

While these tests are by no means foolproof indicators of what your candidate will be like on the job, they can provide valuable information. Remember: while there are many different personality types, none is more 'superior' than the others. They are all equal, yet different – but this does mean that some personality types are better suited to particular careers than the others.

It has been theorized that the ENFP and ENFJ types are naturally inclined towards empathy, listening, communication and teamwork. These traits make for excellent sales people, and we are always on the lookout for individuals who fall into these categories.

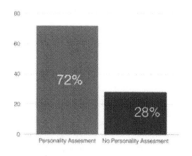

source- 2016 trends report from business advisory company CEB

Did you know that 72% of all companies today implement personality assessments before hiring? This is substantial! Only 28% don't do any personality testing. Take note that personality testing is proven to be a vital part of the hiring process of the Fortune 500.

The personality tests are the more accurate measure of a salesperson and will determine if the candidates are likely to be a good fit for the company. As you get to know the different personality types, you're going to know who you won't need or those that will be assets.

How it all began

Ironically, I realized the need for personality tests after emailing an event producer I had hired. After sending him an email, I sat and waited for a response because I knew he read it (I got the "read" receipt). He didn't answer, and that drove me nuts! To me, not responding right away meant he was disrespectful and didn't care about what I had to say. I could not understand this behavior.

In correspondence, my personality type is - I get an email, I read it, and I answer it right away. On the other hand, his personality type is - he reads the email, he thinks about it, he reads it again, he sleeps on it, he reads it again and, finally, he answers. Ugh! In the beginning, I thought this was crazy but I came to realize there's no right or wrong way here. We are all different, and that was how *he* did things.

When I accepted his personality type, I understood he wasn't disrespecting me. It was his way of processing information. This is a prime example of two different personality types working together and that's why I believe personality tests are essential when you're building a team, especially a sales team.

The relationship you have with the salesperson must be the strongest relationship in the company.

Using the Brenda story as an example, the best advice is to take advantage of Personality Tests. The results will amaze you. That's guaranteed. The key to this test is giving the first answer that comes to mind and not overthinking the questions. Additionally, you should avoid people who mirror your personality type. My first two hires were people exactly like me. That explained why we fought all the time. Build a team with individuals of various skill sets that would make a cohesive team.

In the special event industry, most are in it because they have a passion for what they do like they love baking or cooking or fashion designing or creating an opportunity for others. Whatever they do, they do because they have a passion for it.

Landing a sale is different. Not everyone has the talent for it. This is when we should look closely at who comprises the whole team and make sure we have the right sales people who can close a deal.

THE INTERVIEW

Preparing for the salesperson's job interview

A truly wise salesperson will prepare for the interview by researching the potential employer. The applicant will be able to give a brief history of the business, highlight achievements and mention any awards or honors the company may have received in the past.

By showing they have done their homework, they are telling the employer they value the opportunity to work for the company. This is exactly the kind of impression you want your sales person to make on the clients.

A well-prepared sales professional, while attending the interview, listens carefully to the questions and then demonstrates their knowledge with a thoughtful answer. This person is one who prepares to meet the clients and is a possible candidate for the job. In addition, a role play scenario can be a determining factor. Later in this book, find out how role play can assist you in selecting the best salesperson for the job.

Right before the interview

After narrowing your search for the best job applicant to compatible sales candidates, it is time to schedule interviews. As an employer, prepare for the interview just as vigorously as you expect your candidate to do so. Carefully select questions aiming at personality traits suited for the sales job and consider using role play as a portion of the interview.

The Interview

We have arrived at the interview stage, and the applicants must answer questions face-to-face. After the initial phone screening and tests, the respondents are expected to come fully prepared to answer questions that may come from all angles.

Ask the right questions and expect the right answers

By asking a sales candidate, "How did you prepare for this interview today?" you can reap a wealth of information about work ethics. Were they caught off-guard by the question? Did they meet it with composure and preparedness? Ideally, the answer will impress you as being well thought out.

One potential salesperson might tell you about their personal care regime; "I ate a proper meal, got a full night's sleep and carefully chose my attire," while others might panic or give you a blank stare. These and body language will reveal the way they handle pressure.

After feeling the applicants are prepared for the interview, we can now file questions they were not prepared for; so we can see how they answer on the spot. I never gave these questions away or even asked them in the survey or the personality test.

• Have you ever worked with someone you did not get along with as part of the team? How did you handle the situation? They have to answer like that?

• What is more important, loyalty or honesty? This is a hard question. How are they going to answer that? This is how you see if the candidates are on their toes if they can answer questions they may not know the answers to as sales people.

•We are interviewing a large group of great candidates for this position. Why should we choose you? This question is one you can leave out because it's a question they are prepared for. It's interesting to hear what they have to say though.

- What did you see about this company that convinced you that you would like to work here?

- Sell yourself to me in 2 minutes. Go! People may struggle with this one but it's a good test to see how they are under pressure

- How do you handle multiple tasks coming from multiple managers?

- What are your short-term and long-term career goals?

The above questions will give you a fairly good idea who you're interviewing. You can get the essence of who they are with them.

To find a true salesperson

You don't have to ask all of these questions in a single interview session. The interview should be casual and comfortable. On the day it's nice weather, try conducting the interview outside on the office grounds, hoping they feel comfortable enough to reveal the true person you're going to hire.

When the interview takes place in an office, some candidates feel uptight knowing they're being tested for a job as a salesperson. Picture the nervous candidates in the waiting area. You sense what's about to happen but attempt to make them feel comfortable. An attempt to make them feel comfortable would be a step in the right direction. We don't want to set them up for failure. The more relaxed they are, the better it will be to see how they react to unexpected situations.

Another tricky question is "What are some things your current employer could do differently to become more successful?" The reason is so powerful because applicants who speak negatively about their past employer you may want to think twice before inviting them to your company.

If they respond with good suggestions like, "I noticed the warehouse workers were unloading the trucks this way, and I thought there might be a better way." Those answers are constructive and could provide help to the company. It is amazing what you can discover by asking the right questions. With the right queries and techniques, you're on the road to getting a Brenda, not the impostor but the real Brenda.

From placing a strong recruitment listing to creating an interview process that works for your company, these are just some of the strategies that can be used. It is important that you craft and hone these suggestions to fit your business – but as a basic template, this is a great place to start.

To reiterate:

During the interview
Now that you have narrowed your candidate list down
to those who are best suited to your position, it is time
to schedule interviews. As an employer, you should
prepare for the interview just as vigorously as you
would expect your candidate to do so. Carefully select
targeted questions, and consider crafting a role-playing
scenario.

**Ask the right questions – and look for the right
answers**

Asking a candidate, the seemingly simple question,
"how did you prepare for this interview today?" can
reap a wealth of information about their work ethic. Do
they seem caught off by this question, or are they
composed and prepared? Ideally, you are looking for an
individual who has a polished and well thought out
answer.

While some people might tell you about their personal
care regime (I ate healthily, got a full night's sleep and
carefully chose my attire), others might blank and look
panicked. This will tell you a lot about how they deal
under pressure when a client asks them an unexpected
candidate.

A truly gifted salesperson will tell you that they have
prepared for your interview by researching your
company. They will be able to give you a brief history
of your business, highlight your achievements and

19

mention any awards or honors you have received in the past. By showing you that they have done their homework, they are telling you that they value your time and that they are serious about the opportunity to work for your company.

This is exactly the kind of impression that you want a top salesperson to make on your clients. A sales professional that comes to meetings well prepared, listens carefully to questions and then demonstrates their knowledge with a thoughtful answer – this is who you want out there in the world, representing your brand.

"The Fairy Job Mother"

First, let me just give you the back story of *The Fairy Job Mother*. Does anybody remember this show? This was a television show I think made during the recession or right after it. People were looking for jobs, so there was this "job nanny" going to interviews with the job seekers and helping them.

In the video, a woman comes in for her interview to be an event planner. Of course, the idea is to plant unhappy clients, and she is asked to 'take care' of them to prove herself. She did well at first and seemed to be in control; however, she became emotional and started to cry because it brought back memories. She failed the interview. The applicant responded well otherwise, scored major points for having done the research and having the experience in solving problems. She blew it though.

Here is the transcript of the show:

Feastivities has come up with a very effective way of finding out the capability of an applicant in handling stressful Events situations. As part of the interview, the applicant is presented with a real life situation of a client who isn't happy with the way the Event is being set-up so far. This is a test on how the aspirant can turn the situation around.

The Applicant, Janelle, was in a position where she was in danger of losing her house and direly needed to be successful in passing this interview. She just had to get this job. She started out very positive, quite articulate in answering Meryl Snow's question on how she prepared for the interview. That she looked up the company, knew that the company was in existence for 22 years, therefore stable, and knew that Meryl Snow was recognized as one of the industry leaders when it came to event planning. She did her homework!

However, Meryl mentioned that her resume was impressive, yes, but that there was nothing about event planning at all in it. Janelle's response was that her skill gained from working in television was transferrable. That the need to calm down on TV for the first time, was no different from calming down a bride-to-be who might be getting a little stressed about planning the biggest party of her life. That made sense and was reasonable.

When the question on what were her monumental screw-ups was asked, her answer was spot-on too! She didn't see them as screw-ups but as learning experiences: to expect the unexpected and to always have a contingency plan in place, so as not to lose direction; to fix what needed fixing, and quickly.

All good, so far. Then Meryl's assistant came in announcing the arrival of an unsatisfied couple, upon entrance, was they were clearly upset and arguing. The fictitious situation (with the role playing done by Christopher and Dan actual Feastivities Event Producers) was that Christopher felt like the Daniel was ruining his entire vision for their wedding.

Christopher wanted it to be a cocktail event and didn't want to assign seating. He explained that he didn't want that kind of energy. Meryl unexpectedly asked if Janelle could answer the question, followed by Daniel's response that if she could tell them how to pay for $6,000 worth of lounge furniture.

Janelle took the cue, stood up and said that, in behalf of Feastivities, she would do whatever it took to resolve the issue. The applicant suggested to take a little off the flowers and the food so money could be directed where the client wanted it to go, to shift things around a little bit and compromise. Daniel butted in, saying he wanted Christopher to get what he wanted. Christopher, on the other hand, didn't believe that, because Daniel was making it very difficult for him to get what he wanted.

Janelle asked them both to put themselves in her shoes for a second. She started getting emotional and went on to say that she had been without a job for 2 years and didn't have the luxury of being able to buy a $6000 chair, or flowers, or spend money and have people fly in to see her. She said she was at the point where she was about to lose everything that she had and that all she had left was her family and people who cared about her. She clearly lost it and broke down, having associated her misfortune to the event, bringing into the mix her stress and emotional baggage. In the process, she lost Christopher who said he didn't want to get wrapped up in all that.

The interview ended with Meryl advising Janelle against being emotional on the job, that it's all about the client, that they need their planner to be a rock and not break down in difficult situations. So, it was down to the gentle brush off: "I shall review this and talk to the other team members and we'll get back to you and give you a call".

You can view the actual footage on
www.youtube.com/merylsnow
(search FJM video)

The point is - if you do something unexpected at job interviews, some people will perform the task at hand while others will crumble. Will the latter really happen? Not knowing the planned surprise and being taken out of one's comfort zone, there's a good chance it will. We've seen how the test works, and it does work very, very well.

CHAPTER 2

Salesperson Contract/Agreement

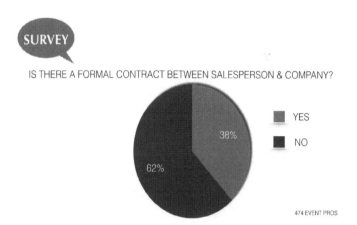

SURVEY

IS THERE A FORMAL CONTRACT BETWEEN SALESPERSON & COMPANY?

YES

NO

38%

62%

474 EVENT PROS

Is there a formal contract between a salesperson and the company? 474 event professionals were asked this, and 62% said "no." How many have a contract between the company and the salesperson? Even with the majority giving a negative response, it's not enough to say that a contract's not necessary.

A contract is important as it protects you and it protects the employee. You can't go into this with eyes wide

25

shut because it's a relationship. You should have a mutually-beneficial relationship on paper. Not everybody knows what the rules are, right? So, let's do this. The employee agreement is in six steps, and it's at-will.

The employee agreement

There are several points to be covered. The agreement is composed of job responsibilities, work hours, salary commission, confidential information, and the benefits. The following areas are most common for companies to focus on:

- Code of conduct
- Confidentiality
- Hours and compensation
- Working conditions
- Leave requirements

*** check with your lawyer

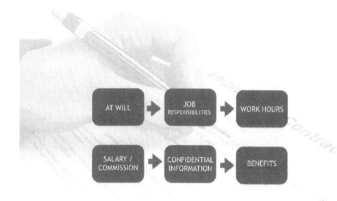

Employee at will

"Nothing in this agreement will change the employer/employee relationship between the salesperson in the company and that of an employee at will. Either the company or you may terminate your employment for any reason at any time and without notice or further obligation, according to the terms set forth in section 5."

Job responsibilities

"Your job responsibilities shall be described to you by the company from time to time and shall include but not limited to the job description." And here's the big thing - "The sales plan which you have designed is also incorporated into this agreement and job description."

27

So, what we're asking them to do is to write their duties and explain how they are going to achieve their goals.

Work hours

"Work hours shall be a minimum of 40 hours per week Monday through Friday, and/or such other or additional hours as shall be scheduled in connection with your performance of scheduled events and meetings during evenings and weekends."

Salary and commission

"Base draw against commission. Your base draw shall be $100,000 per year which shall be payable bi-weekly. Commissions - All sales are calculated on Synergy (Synergy is our computer software) prices at the time of sale on commissionable sales of $1 million dollars and above. Feastivities will pay you a 10% commission on food bar set ups, in-house equipment, labor, and rentals." Consequently, we pay commission on everything except for tax and delivery.

Salary commissions and sales contests

"This commission will be paid on a commission of all sales of over $1 million dollars and only after the event has been sold and orchestrated to completion by you. The company shall pay your commission bi-weekly but only after the company has received full payment for the catering function to which your commissions relate.

As your sales exceed $1 million dollars, you will need to advise on how you exceeded the sales goal and verified with the Controller. Your draw will be increased to match your earned commissions. "There will be no commission paid on contracts that are not assigned and paid in full. Commissions will be paid in the payroll check in the pay period following the company receiving a full payment and your submittal of your commission worksheet. In addition, your commission shall be calculated only on the total cost to the client of any catering function and shall not be calculated on tax delivery and gratuities.

Furthermore, The Company shall have the right to assign sales leads to its sales personnel at its sole discretion, and also at its sole discretion designate which catering function shall be priced at a mark-up that is lower than the standard mark-up." This means we're protecting ourselves. What we're doing is taking away all the gray areas - protecting the employee and protecting the company. When things are written out in advance, they know the rules. There is nothing worse than someone saying, "I didn't know that."

This protects you: "In the event, the Producer/Planner makes a pricing mistake (I hear 'what if they make a mistake?' all the time) that negatively affects the regularly published pricing, that amount will be deducted from their earned commission of the sale. Furthermore, any mistake due to negligence on the producer's part, resulting in unforeseen additional costs to the company, will negatively affect the commission on the sale and the amount of the additional cost incurred.

Refunds and reimbursements

Now, let's say an event producer forgot to order chairs and you need chairs for the event. This will only happen once and one time only. You will call a rental company and have them bring chairs over. Not only do you have a double delivery charge same day in and out, plus the rental of the chairs because they didn't charge the client, but it's a mistake committed by the event planner and deducted from their commission.

Next, let's say they ordered the chairs and they weren't delivered. You now have to call another rental company and get those chairs. In this case, who pays for that? Not the salesperson as she did her job. The company pays for it meantime and then you will get it back from the rental company. It wouldn't be the sales person's problem. The company absorbs it. If the sales person makes a mistake, they're responsible for that. If a mistake has happened, or you have to give the money back to the client for whatever reason, that is not their responsibility; the company absorbs it. That's only fair; it's fair to all.

But when the money is given back because the food ran out, this is not the sales person's fault as she did her job. She should still get her commission. When there is an argument back and forth with the salespeople and the owner on commissions, that's the worst thing in the world. This could ruin your relationship forever.

Other commissions

"Non-standard markups such as musicians, decorators, florists, entertainment, games will be marked up 40% of the cost of the item including the sales tax. You will receive 3% commission on the marked-up price excluding tax and delivery (unless the delivery is marked up 40% as well)."

Jobs less than published prices

"In the event, the company designates a price markup for a catering function less than the standard markup, the commission percentage set above shall not apply. Instead, you and the company shall agree to a reduced commission for that type of event, like fundraisers, and pro bono, like an open house. We reserve the right, in its sole discretion, to exclude commissions altogether on such events" We can't pay commissions when there were some sales where no money was paid.

Sales contest

"To encourage the achievement of goals, the company may hold several sales contests throughout the year with awards of bonus checks, gift certificates or other prizes. Those who accomplish or exceed their goals, awards may be given at various levels." They get excited about this.

Confidential information

"You understand during the course of your employment, you are likely to become familiar with the secret propriety or confidential information of the company such as, but not limited to, a list of clients, specific information regarding such clients, types and kinds of event arrangements, list of suppliers and equipment, etc."

This protects the employer. A company who did not have a contract in place lost her business because of it.

Her sales people started a catering business and took her clients with them. It can happen. The business crumbled. She only found out what happened when she saw the letterhead of the new company left in the copier. Her sales people were running their business in her company!

I can't stress enough how important a contract is. Without it, you stand to lose. The contract goes on to say:

"While employed advice, equate the knowledge you hear, if your employment with the company is terminated, whether voluntary or involuntary, surrender all books, etc. You agree not to become an employee of an independent contractor or a consultant or do any work in exchange for compensation or without compensation as an account executive, sales person or event planner for another catering company within 60 miles."

Some people say non-competes won't hold up in court. Well, sometimes, they do. Most of the time they will favor the employee because you can't stop somebody from making a living; however, most of the employees who sign the contract believe the non-compete will hold.

Benefits

The 401K and their vacations are explained. Normally, new hires are given one week vacation after one year and, after two years, they are allowed to take two weeks of relaxation. The employees must schedule their vacation time. That said, there is always an exception to the rule: if the company is not busy. In addition, the months of May, June, September, October, and December are not open for leaves.

Chapter 3

Compensation

Let's talk about compensation. Some employers pay hourly, salary plus commission, all commission or draw. I typically stay away from all commission, the last thing they should be thinking about is worrying about paying their car payment or mortgage.

An example of Draw:

Event Producer can do up to 950, -1M in sales by themselves. After that, they need an assistant (Event Planner)

Sales people will pay for themselves with this scenario:

Commission Structure: Draw (all commission) industry standard is 6-10% of all sales (with the proper mark-up) excluding tax.

For the sake of ease, I will use 10% as an example. The company never pays more than the established percentage. The reason to use Draw is the sales people can still have a set income without the ebbs & flows.

Example: Sales Rep with assistant

Sales 1.5M

Draw 150K

The 150K is divided into 12 months=12.5K

Producer receives 70% of 12.5K

Planner receives 30% of 12.5K

When they reach their sales goals- usually later in the year the draw continues however they will receive an additional 10% on sales after the 1.5M goal.

If they don't reach their sales goals, then the draw needs to be adjusted accordingly. This is very important to view the numbers with sales people monthly.

COMPENSATION

Slow hire or fast hire?

By now you probably know not to hire anyone hastily. In the next segment, learn how to train, mentor, and motivate your sales people. Now that you've hired your team, you've got to train them properly.

CHAPTER 4

Training A Salesperson

Role playing can test your candidate's mettle

Sometimes the best way to assess your candidate's abilities is to watch them in action. I have our employees pose as disgruntled clients during a salesperson interview. First, they pretend to demand to see me, and when I allow them access to the meeting, they express a few pointed concerns.

I then ask the candidate to field the concerns and intervene, as if they are already in the position. They are not pre-warned about this exercise – I truly want to see them on their toes and in an unexpected situation that they could not have planned for in advance.

Not only do I get to see how well my candidate does under fire, but this exercise also shows them that working for my company will be a dynamic and exciting experience. No two days are ever the same, and that is why I don't simply want someone who is adept at answering stock interview questions. I want to know that they are a creative and exciting thinker who can handle a sticky client situation and turn it around quickly and professionally.

If they break down, fumble too much with their words, completely 'blank' out or otherwise fail this test, you can rest assured that they will not be able to handle the complexities of an event when the time comes. Remember – even the best plans can fail, and when a client emergency occurs you need someone who can appease the situation, save the sale and make your company look good.

Policies & Procedures:

Policies and procedures are vital to the productivity of an organization. It ensures the employee knows what is expected of them and what their responsibilities are. P&P narratives are also essential in that they provide key criteria that an employee can expect to be evaluated on.

Without a clear description being agreed upon by an employer and an employee, confusion and disagreements can develop.

Well-written policies and procedures bring structure to any business, no matter what the size.

CHA CHING

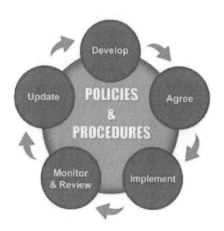

Policy & Procedure Example:

#_714

POLICY AND PROCEDURE MANUAL

SUBJECT: Commissions – Team of Three

Objective:

To provide an equitable arrangement to our Sales Producers and Event Planners (Primary and Secondary) for growing the company revenues

Policy:

On each contract signed and paid in full, the commission is 10% of Total Sales before Venue fees, Sales Tax, Delivery or Gratuity and after all discounts are applied. Of this 10% on

Spread Sheet is to be submitted to the VP – Sales for approval and then submitted to the Controller by the Monday following the 1st of each month for verification and adjustment to base draw or payment. This commission is due ONCE the Sales Producer and Event Planner exceeds their base draw amount ((Base Draw is estimated by using 6% or 2.85% or 1.15%) of projected sales as applies). As their base draw amount is exceeded they need to advise VP - Sales of how they have exceeded their base draw in order to increase their pay based on commission, this will be verified by the Controller. There will be no commission paid on contracts that are not signed and paid in full.

Any deviation to this policy must be approved by

                    Effective 7-19-16

Training Manual

According to Dale Carnegie, companies whose employees are well engaged outperform their competitors by over 200%. Employee engagement is not possible without employee training; it follows that having a good employee training manual in place can help boost your company's ability to engage its employees.

Creating quality training manuals for various positions in a company is an important part of the organization's talent management plan. When training manuals are available for key positions in a company, it is possible to ensure continuity of operations when new employees are hired, and it sure does stop the questions on "How do I do…"

Taking time to write out an employee training manual may seem like a laborious task. However, a formal training manual ensures consistency in the presentation of the training program. Another major advantage is that all the training information on skills, processes, and other information necessary to perform the tasks is together in one place. Training manuals should support the training objectives.

Tips on starting a manual:

- The best way to start a training manual is to place yourself in the training process.
- Have a recording device and dictate at the moment an employee pulls into the parking lot. (Where are they to park? Which door do they enter? Where is the time clock? Do they need to put the heat on?
- Assign other team members to create a portion of the training manual. For example, you may have someone that has mastered the company software programs.
- Maximize employee engagement: Your manual will benefit if you include:
  - **Be Clear & Concise**– avoid information overload
  - **The combination of text and visual aids** – use images, illustrations, tables, diagrams etc.

- o **Logical structure** – headings, page numbers, section summaries and tab dividers etc.
- o **Write in the active sense:** Active sentences tend to be shorter and less confusing. Passive sentences tend to be longer and more confusing.

- o **Well formatted** – visually pleasing, color coded, good use of white space and generous margins to accommodate note taking
- o **Regular intervals** – Q&A sections, worksheets, learning checklists and quizzes.

- Training manual content should be based on objectives so it is possible to tell when trainees have mastered the material.

Below is an example of a training manual for the special event industry:

Table of Contents

- Office Policies & Procedures
- Opening & Closing the Office Check List
- Computer Tips
- Calendar Sharing
- Office Phone System – Handling Calls
- Office Phone System – Setting up Voice Mail
- Office Phone System – Using Voice Mail
- Office Phone System – Miscellaneous Tips
- Planner & Producer Check List
- Inquiry
- 1st Meeting Guidelines with Scripts
- An Event from Start to Finish
- Terms & Conditions (T&C) Contracts
- Deposit Schedules & Payment Reminders

- Scheduling Meeting
- Shop Tour & Scripts
- Tasting & Meeting Calendar
- Setting up Meeting Rooms
- On the Street Tracking
- Proposals & Contracts
- Rentals & Linens
- Weekly Planner Tasks
- AC/Heat Requests
- Vendor Meals
- Printing for Masters
- Vendor Confirmations
- Final Invoices
- Packing Lists
- General Packing List Sheet
- Event Paperwork & Signs
- Synergy – Software Training

CHAPTER 5

Coaching & Mentoring A Sales Person

Survey:

The main purpose of in-house sales surveys is to know what your team needs to work on and to decipher what their current issues may be.

Using surveys to collect this information can give valuable insights into areas such as sales techniques, problem-solving and adherence to policies & procedures.

MERYL SNOW

* 1. What is your name & title? 🔲

[   ]

2. How long have you been with the company? 🔲

○ 1-2 years
○ 3-5 years
○ 6-10 year
○ 11 & over

* 3. Rank client reasons for not booking the event.
(1-7) 1 being most often 🔲

∷	⬥	Heard negative comments / reviews
∷	⬥	Chose another venue
∷	⬥	Price
∷	⬥	Food better at other caterers tasting
∷	⬥	Not having the event

* 4. There are times in the sales process that a client asks a question or a statement that you may stumble in addressing or would like another way to answer it.

Please list five 🔲

[   ]

* 5. My favorite part of my job is... 🔲

[   ]

* 6. My least favorite part of my job is... 🔲

[   ]

7. After the initial inquiry, I send a proposal to a client even though I don't believe they will book. 🔲

○ True
○ False

Why?
[   ]

CHA CHING

* 8. My best line for closing the sale is...

```
[                                            ]
```

9. Rank yourself on these skills
(1 to 6) with 1 being your greatest strength.

⠿	[◆]	Bonding with client
⠿	[◆]	Closing the sale
⠿	[◆]	Event planning / logistics
⠿	[◆]	Qualifying client

* 10. I always address our competition in the sales process.

◯ True

◯ False

Why?

```
[                                            ]
```

49

* 11. List 5 benefits of why clients should use our company. 🔲

* 12. What are 4 ways to qualify a client? 🔲

* 13. How do you keep connected with past clients to book future events? 🔲

* 14. If you could change three things about your role, what would they be? 🔲

* 15. What two additional tools could the company provide for you? 🔲

* 16. Do you spend some amount of work time regularly prospecting for new business? 🔲

○ Always

○ Sometimes

○ Rarely

○ Never

* 17. Who are your top three Competitors? 🔲

[Done]

COMPLACENCY— THE ENEMY OF A SUCCESSFUL TEAM

Slumps in your level of motivation are a natural phenomenon. Lack of motivation, however, can have dire financial consequences such as reduction in profit. Motivated sales people sell more, no doubt. Going about your business looking like the weight of the world is on your shoulders has never helped anyone boost their sales. Attitude and mindset play significant roles in enabling you to reach targets and shoot your company to the heights you desire.

Complacency is the enemy of success. It is easy to become complacent over time, never pushing oneself and ceasing to go an 'extra mile' for the sake of your company and clients. Without a doubt, you know that you need to be motivated to succeed at sales, you want to be motivated but you find out that you just cannot attain and maintain that motivation. Is this the case?

Motivation is an in-house job; it begins and ends with you. Even if you fail to realize it, motivation is something you can control, an internal job. No one gets to determine your level of motivation. You need to take responsibility for your motivation – every second, every minute, hourly and daily. While it is good to source for inspiration from motivational speakers, workshops, and mantras, the drive to increase sales must come from within you. Rekindling motivation starts with bearing in mind the reason why you started your company in the first place. Doubts and other issues can make you lose sight of why you started and your initial passion. It is the passion for what you do and an unreserved belief in what you're selling that drives you to win clients over at the end of the day. Review the thank-you letters, calls, publicity and awards you have received from satisfied clients and rekindled that passion for what you do! It goes a long way in renewing your enthusiasm for selling.

Motivating a team is one of the most important things that a leader can do. Without guidance, employees can fail and suffer, unsure of what to do next and how to succeed to their highest potential. While it is true that no one can truly motivate anyone (true gumption has to come from within), a good leader can do a tremendous amount to influence people and encourage their motivation and success.

Part of keeping your team motivated and excited about always improving is also ensuring that they don't become complacent. We all know the type: arrive at work in a daze, clock in, and then sit at their desk doing the bare minimum to get by. Then, they leave as early as possible, never really committing to their career path, and worst of all—detract from, rather than add to, the success of the team. If these types are already satisfied with what they have, it can become increasingly difficult to engage them and motivate them to success.

Why do good people become complacent?

Sometimes even the best workers can become complacent over time. Feeling happy and unfulfilled in their career, some individuals can fall into the habit of quiet complacency, never pushing themselves and ceasing to go that 'extra mile' for their boss or their client. They do this without realizing that their co-workers and manager may be fostering a slowly simmering resentment toward their blasé attitude.

Are competitions motivating your team?

Many managers decide to motivate their teams by setting up competitions and monetary incentives intended to encourage everyone to get back on board and do their very best. Team spirit! While these types of incentives can be a temporary measure that appears to work at first, money is not always the answer. Sometimes the very best motivating factors are interpersonal relationships—caring for the success of the team is an excellent way to boost morale and performance.

Focus on relationships with your team

We all know what it feels like to be managed skillfully versus being managed poorly. If you are in management, know that trying to intimidate your employees into respecting you will not work. A Drill Sargent won't gain their employees' respect.

Instead of barking orders, counteract complacency by celebrating goals and accomplishments. Make a big deal out of it when they make a huge sale or land a new client! By warmly and regularly congratulating your team when they do well (and working on building them up when they are struggling) you will reach goals you have never dreamed of.

Nip negativity: get rid of cancerous employees

Negative employees or CAVE dwellers (Consistently Against Virtually Everything) are a cancer in your organization. They will bring you down and destroy the morale of your other employees. Sometimes you can work with these individuals to get them back on track, but sometimes they just have to go. Conversely, you may have a great employee who just isn't getting the job done, consistently underperforming and bringing the team down. Don't be too quick to dismiss these people— they may simply be in the wrong position in your company. Sit down and ask them, "If I had a magic wand, what position would you like to have in this company?" By listening to your employee, you will learn how to manage them better and bring your entire team to success.

Laugh and play with your team!

Most importantly, you have to remember that we are all social beings. Saying thank you and laughing with your team can go much further toward a harmonious and successful business environment than any competition can. Spend time together, enjoy their company, and listen to what they have to say—these are the steps to managing your team with poise, enjoyment, and skill.

CHAPTER 6

Setting And Tracking Sales Goals

Salespeople are driven by goals

True sales people are driven by goals

The struggle to make sales goal the best it can be and continue on an upward trajectory is one that every company faces. Developing a plan for sales growth as an ongoing activity can improve your sales and sanity.

How to Set Company Goals for Your Special Event Business

For a business, growth is everything. The growth of revenue, the growth of sales – the only things that growth can bring are good ones. It is a word that companies want to be reminded of, and one that they should always keep in mind. However, you cannot achieve growth without having some goals laid out for you to conquer. Of course, when you first start out, things are going to be a little quiet and possibly even disheartening – but you need to persevere through it.

As the owner of your business, it is up to you to determine the sales goals that you want to hit and to ensure that they are realistic. While it will be hard, in the beginning, it will get easier as time goes by. Here is how to set company goals for your special event business in a clear and effective manner.

Discover Your Sales Cycle

This is not as vague as it may sound. A sales cycle is something that every company has, and while it can vary a little depending on your industry, it does tend to have a pretty solid foundation. A typical sales cycle looks a little like this:

- Introductory call

- Conversation with potential client

- An Appointment with the potential client

-   Demonstration of product and/or abilities

-   The proposal

-   Closing the sale/deal

As previously mentioned, the stages can vary, and you may find that your company has fewer stages (or possibly more) than those listed above. No matter what your sales cycle looks like, it should be used to help you create appropriate and realistic sales goals.

Determine Your Monthly Sales Goal

You also need to determine your monthly sales goal. This is the amount you would like to see coming into your company each month. One of the easiest ways to calculate this is to take your annual goal and cut it into quarters. Of course, for some entertainment industries, this might not be the best route as they have peak seasons for business. If this is the case, you may need to alter your monthly goal so that it works nicely alongside your peak seasons.

You also need to decide what is included in your monthly sales goal. Does it include all of your products or just the main ones that sell the best? Are your sales reps going to be able to make the numbers? Leading on from this point, you also have to remember that some reps will be better than others, just as they will all have different strengths and weaknesses. Make sure that you remember this before you set your sales goals each month.

Create Goals for Productivity

Productivity is key, whether you have a team of sales reps or you are working on your own. Without productivity, there can be no growth, and your company will eventually collapse. Creating goals for you or your team to work towards is an excellent incentive but also helps you to lay out clear goals that work on anything from a daily basis to a monthly one.

You can have software installed on your company computers where your sales reps will log their calls and sales as they make them. This will help you to determine who your best employees are, but also the general levels of productivity that your staff is currently achieving. It will help you to better understand your sales cycle, as well as things you can do to boost the productivity levels of your staff. Make sure you always discuss new goals with your team first and raise the expected amount slowly so as not to overwhelm and pressure them too much.

Make Sure Your Goals are Realistic

It is so important to set realistic goals for your company. Setting unrealistic expectations leads to you being disappointed when they are not met, and your sales team feeling disheartened and stressed when they aren't able to make them either. Take a look at your company and think about your annual goals. Are they realistic?

You also need to assess the market potential. Is there room for you and your company to grow, and if there is an untapped area, can you get it before others come and take their share? Aggressive sales early on can be just what your business needs to thrive, but not every business will benefit from it. Looking for nuances in the market and little corners that have not been touched will also help you to see if there is space for your business in the market, helping you to see things from a more realistic point of view.

Never Forget the Long-Term Goals

Your long-term goals are just as important as the ones you are setting yourself on a monthly (or even daily) basis. It is the long-term goals that will help you grow, as each of the short-term ones that are completed builds you towards them. When you sit down to plan your goals, think of both the long and short-term ones.

You need a sales team that is committed and ready to get to work, but you also cannot leave them to handle it alone. They need guidance and support when it comes to achieving their goals, and it is your job to do this. Help them to grow and improve so that they can be the best possible team for the growth of your business.

Give Rewards and Incentive to Your Team

Your sales team is important, and they need to be rewarded and given the incentive to keep working as hard as they can and to be the most productive versions of themselves. Create a prize that will be won by the best sales team member, and it will create an atmosphere of friendly competition among your employees. The prize doesn't have to be anything big, just something that will give them a little extra encouragement.

Implementing bonuses and commission are also ways in which you can provide your sales team with a little extra motivation and improve morale. These schemes can be very helpful, and often encourage employees to strive for perfection. Similarly, when you first start your company, you should work directly with your first sales reps. This lets you all understand each other and form a bond, but it also gives them a confidence boost and increases morale.

It won't be easy in the beginning, and you may find that you don't meet them for the first year or so. This is normal, and with persistence and determination, you will make it through stronger on the other side. Set realistic goals, be supportive, and your company will thrive.

A company needs to be sales driven - the white board is an example of sales tracking. Proposals, bookings, goals & sales are tracked for each team every month.

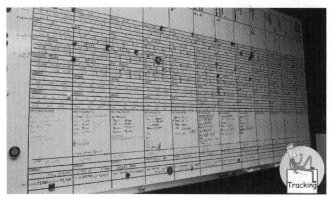

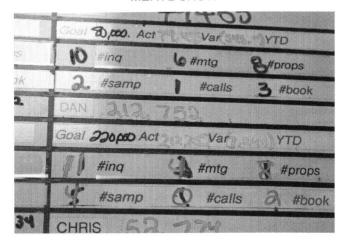

Each team has an Event Producer and one or more Event Planners. The event producer drives the team in sales, meets with the prospective clients and brings them to contract- then the event planner takes over all the details of the event- paperwork, ordering and client communications to the events fruition. This concept releases the Event Producer to go after more sales. The team is paid a 10% commission on all sales except for tax & delivery.

An example: from the 10% commission, the event producer is paid 7% and the event planner 3%. If another event planner is added to the team the 10% rule still applies, and the percentages are recalculated.

A rule of thumb- one event producer & one planner can easily do over 1.8 million in sales.

This scenario is the draw method for payment. Assuming 1 million in sales goal- we take the 10% model which is $100,000. 70% or $70,000 is allocated to the event producer. That 70,000 is split between 12 months as their draw. When sales go beyond the million, they will continue to receive their draw plus commission over the goal.

A sales manager's job is to individually coach each member of his or her sales team to their fullest potential. In-depth 1-on-1 sales tracking session should be done in person with each sales person every other week. This conversation takes about 20 to 30 minutes and is very focused on goals, pipeline, meetings, and proposals. It is also a way to address issues a salesperson may be facing. This time allows you to coach and mentor practical and relevant sales skills.

A meeting that neglects to define what achievement looks like and the reasonable action steps expected to arrive is not a productive use of time. By holding routine meetings, you'll have the ability to spot issues early on.

Sales questions for Sales Tracking Meeting

1. How much money is out on the street in proposals?
2. How qualified is the event on a scale of 1-5?
3. Where are they in the sales process?
4. What's their definitive next step?

CHAPTER 7

You Don't Need A Laser Show To Run An Effective Sales Meeting

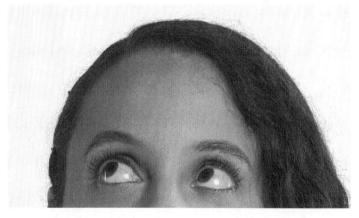

Let's face it – if your sales force is anything like most other companies when they realize it is time for the weekly sales meeting, they may cringe. We have all been there – sitting through monotone speakers with PowerPoint presentations that go on for slide after slide about updates, motivation and the keys to success. The problem is that a lot the information you get out of these meetings is not very helpful when it comes time for the staff to go out and try to snag new jobs and contracts. While you do not need to go out and get celebrity guest stars, have a Pink Floyd laser show or bribe everyone with free breakfast to show up, there are some things you can do to run an effective sales meeting, no matter how big or small the meeting may be.

Here Comes the Morning Eye Roll

You see it happen all of the time and it may even happen to you when you are running the meeting. So much of what can go on at a sales meeting can just bring a sense of dread over most of the people in attendance that it is frightening. The sales meeting does not have to be something that everyone tries to avoid like the plague, yet it happens week after week. Just why is there so much dread about your meetings? More than likely it is because of things like:

- **The Meeting is Unorganized** – Everyone gets into the meeting room and there is no structure to the meeting at all. With no agenda, it is hard for anyone to stay on point and stay focused.
- **Going Off on Tangents** – This happens all of the time at meetings. Someone starts to go off on a tangent that is completely unrelated to the topic being discussed and it completely derails the whole meeting for everyone.
- **Rehashing of Old Items** – When you spend twenty minutes each week talking about the

same things and never getting to the new information and topics it can make the meeting completely unproductive for everyone involved.

So how are you supposed to avoid any of these things from happening and make it, so the sales force wants to have these meetings each week? There are some great solutions that you can try to help keep things on track and make these meetings productive, fun and something the staff looks forward to.

Staying the Course – Planning Your Meeting

There are a couple of basics you want to start with when it comes to planning the sales meeting that will help you. Keep in mind things like:

- **Start and End Times** – Your sales force is likely working on a tight schedule, just like you. They have calls to make, clients to see, contracts to handle and more. Make sure that the meeting has a start time that works well in everyone's schedule most of the time, has a definitive end time and that you stick to both as best as possible all of the time.

- **Keep it Timely** – While you certainly do not need to have a three-hour sales meeting each week, it needs to be more than ten minutes if you want it to really be productive. Set aside an hour for the meeting so it gives you time to cover all of the things you need to get to. You do not want to spend time simply re-hashing everything that went on at this past weekend's event; your operations meeting can take care of all of that. Instead make this hour about information, teaching, inspiration, and ways to achieve goals.

- **Choose the Right Day** – Having your meeting on Monday morning is probably the worst time for you and your sales staff. Everyone likely needs Monday to try to catch up after the weekend and really does not have the time or energy to devote to a meeting right away. Friday can be just as bad as everyone is going to be swamped with all they have to do for the events planned for the weekend. Pick a day in the middle of the week at a time when everyone typically has a lull in schedule to make it happen.

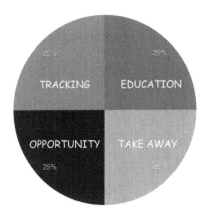

Your Sales Meeting in Four Acts

You can break down your meeting into four 15-minute blocks that will work well for everyone, keep the meeting moving and make it productive. Try a set up like this:

- **Tracking** – Don't start off your sales meetings on a down note. You want to make the meetings a positive experience, so use the first fifteen minutes as a way to praise everyone for the numbers they had during the past week. Congratulate individuals for hitting and exceeding particular sales goals. Make it a big deal because, well, it is a big deal! A round of applause from the group is a great thing for motivation. You can even use this time to do something like hand out gift cards as recognition for great work. For those that may have missed their goals last week, now is not the time for chastising or reprimands. They know they missed the mark already and with the right motivation will strive to do better.

- **Opportunities** – There are sales opportunities all around you all of the time, so devoting fifteen minutes for everyone to share ideas and leads can be ideal. Have each person bring a sale that they want to go after that week to the meeting. It could be something like an advertisement about the new mall coming to the area and how they want to go after the bid to handle the grand opening event. Maybe it is a gala they had bid on and did not get this year and want to go after it again. This is a good time to share that information.

- **Education** – Your sales meeting is a great teaching moment so don't let it just slip by. Take fifteen minutes to go over different sales techniques that can be effective, do some role playing so that the sales force can see how to work with different clients and situations, talk about how to build solid relationships and make a proposal or teach the best way to work on closing a deal. The information learned here can be a big help to your team.

- **The Big Take-Away** – Take the last fifteen minutes to go around the table and let everyone say what the best takeaway from the meeting is for them. The key to doing this is that each person must say something different and not repeat someone else's answer. It will make everyone think about the meeting and what worked best for them and they can get important points reinforced to them by others, helping them retain more information.

Your Role in This

Your role in the meeting each week is very important as the facilitator. Make sure the meeting starts and ends on time each week no matter what. If for some reason the meeting has to be cancelled because of an event make sure you reschedule it for that same week. If you cannot be there for some reason, have another staff member fill in as the facilitator. There may be times where a particular topic needs to run longer for greater emphasis, so let the team know about it so they can adjust their schedules before the meeting.

It is your job as the leader to make sure the sales meeting is a good one each week. Encourage everyone to participate all of the time so the meeting can be more productive for each person. You want your team to feel excited about going to the sales meeting each week and leave the meeting each week feeling inspired to do a great job. Don't be afraid to assign homework from the meeting as well for the next meeting so people can think about and be ready for the next time. Once the meeting is over, arrange the time to meet with each salesperson one-on-one for about fifteen minutes each. This gives each individual time with you to ask questions, get advice, talk about strategies for new business, tweak individual techniques and go over their numbers.

Sales meeting do not have to be the groan-inducers or eye-rollers that everyone dreads going to. If you make the meetings purposeful, interesting and inventive, everyone will be sure they can attend each week, and the company will benefit overall.

Role playing –

Role playing is the most difficult for the people that are actually doing the role playing; who does benefit is the audience because they're not on the hot seat. They're able to listen and say, " I would have said something else" or "She should have said this. Those who benefit are the people that are listening. It does get easier as they continue to role play.

10 Role playing Tips:
1. Never make role playing easy. Let them scramble a little bit, that's what it is going to be like in real life.
2. Make it a safe atmosphere.
3. Add some fun.
4. Role play by title of buyers - a corporate planner, a bride, a mother of the bride, the bridesmaid that thinks she's an event planner.
5. Split role playing between sales peers and sales management.

6. Make a list of your top ten sales objections prior to sales meeting.
7. Redirect straying conversations back to the sales process. In role playing it always goes off gear somewhere and you've got to bring it back in because people feel uncomfortable and they start talking about other things.
8. Lights, Camera, Action- record the role playing session and have the participants watch it privately, this way they analyse what they would do differently.
9. Debrief with kindness and support.
10. Document strengths and weaknesses.

What if you're a small team of two?

It's still a team; you do exactly the same procedure. When you add a third, fourth, fifth team member, you will have this structure set up. Sales people thrive on schedules, training manuals and policies and procedures,

What if your sales people are scattered in different locations?

Technology is so advanced- there are so many different programs for these reasons.
Here are a few:
1. Skype
2. GoToMeetings

3. Google Hangouts
4. VSee
5. UberConference
6. Webex

TIPs for Your Sales Meeting :

- Never be late
- You set the tone
- Make everyone accountable
- "Pass the Pad" have sales people take turns taking meeting notes and type and distribute to attendees.

My first real job I had was with a large hotel conglomerate. I was a trouble shooter service trainer for locations across the country. I was due for a salary review, and I was very excited because I knew I was good at my job. I'm sitting at the table across from my boss, and he's singing my praises, and I'm thinking "This is it, this is it, this is going to be a big fat raise." And then he says to me, "Unfortunately, I can't give you a raise." "What?" And he continues, "You're not following company policy" "What are you talking about? I am the poster child; I do everything I'm told." And then he pauses a moment and says, "No, you don't. You don't follow our Delta system." "Have I ever been late on anything? Do I always meet my deadlines? Do I ever forget anything?" He said, "It doesn't matter, this is company policy."

The Delta is an organizational system that the company started the year before I was hired. They did teach the system to me. However, I had my system that worked. It's a to-do list formatted this way:

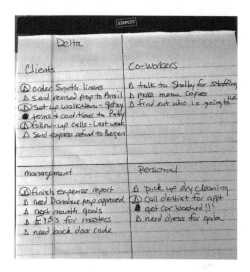

There are four parts – Clients, Co-Workers, Management and Personal.

When something needs to be done, it's placed on the list with a triangle. When the item is in progress a circle is placed around the triangle, and when the project is complete, it's colored in.

For the above example, the Smith linens have been ordered, so it's circled, when the confirmation arrives, then it will be colored in.

A sales person's day is constantly being interrupted, the phone rings, then somebody walks in and tells you to order something, then something else happens. In addition, it sure makes it easy when a co-worker is out sick all you need to do it to look at the list.

The Delta System is a simple yet effective tool for organizing. Keep it to one page and update at the end of each day.

Technology today has many organizational systems, and I've tried them all. But there is just something about the old fashion to-do list (with a little tweak) that just can't be replaced.

CHAPTER 8

Employee Evaluation

EMPLOYEE SELF-EVALUATION FORM

An employee self-evaluation form provides a tool for reviewing past assignments, significant accomplishments, job-related and career development goals, and other topics or problem areas. You will need to provide a copy in advance before your performance review discussion at a mutually agreed upon time.

Time Period Covered:
Employee Name:
Instructions:

PART 1
Please describe your significant job-related accomplishments, the status of last year's performance objectives and future goals. Include a statement regarding job-related training needs and future career plans. The objective of this summary is to provide an opportunity to reflect upon actual work, ensure agreement with your performance regarding accomplishments and priorities, and foster effective communications between both. Attach any additional pages needed to complete this form.

There is no required format.

PART 2
In addition to this exercise, fill out the standard review form.
5 Strengths
5 Areas of Improvement
3 Short Term Goals (1-6 months)
3 Long Term Goals (6 months-1 years)

CHAPTER 9

5 Sales Techniques

Email Inquiries

Qualify

Budget

Cost Analysis

Close

When you're selling YOU, it's important to show your personality: your likes, dislikes, life story, insecurities, and fears. Your ability to market your talents, achievements, and values inside your organization and within your profession, industry, and community are key parts of enhancing your brand.

The most efficient way to promote you is to allow the conversation to become give-and-take. Through natural dialogue, the client will realize that you are intelligent, capable, and have or can acquire the desired skills.

After you return from a meeting with a client, ask yourself: how engaging, relatable, confident, friendly, and trustworthy was I? Learn from every meeting, and continue to improve on how you are portraying your brand and marketing yourself.

TECHNIQUE- EMAIL TO CONVERSATION

If I could just TALK to them
that's all I need

One of the most common remarks I hear from salespeople is, "If I could just talk to them, I know I can book it." A true salesperson knows that having a conversation and building a rapport and trust with the client is paramount.

Today businesses are subject to a multitude of internet inquiries. Years ago, before the World Wide Web, clients would find you from word-of-mouth, from an event that they attended or from print advertising. At that time, you were the expert in your field. When talking or meeting with the client, they could tell how you were different from your competitor just from your photographs, proposals, and ideas.

Now a potential client that is having an event will find you in several ways referral from the venue, word-of-mouth or the Internet, nonetheless, they will most likely go to your website before contacting you, and in turn, they will go to your competitor's website. Regardless of what type of company your competitor is, a good web designer can make a company look perfect. So, in the clients' eyes, you and your competitors are the same. Both websites state that they can accomplish the client's needs and the clients can see themselves using your company, and they could see themselves using your competitor. So that means they are treating you like a commodity and then buy solely on price. The potential client will fill out your contact form and up to six of your competitors as well. Each company is sending the client an email response; some will send photos, some will send videos, some will try to get a meeting. However, all of the competitor emails look alike. To to stand out from the others, you need to be different. Below is a typical email inquiry. Looks familiar – right? Chances are this Bride is sending it to all of your competitors as well.

From: Katie
Sent: Monday, March 07, 2016 8:51 AM
To: Bernk
Subject: Greystone Hall

Good morning,

My fiancé and I are considering having our wedding at Greystone Hall. As you are on the list of preferred vendors, I wanted to reach out and inquire about your catering options/packages, price ranges, and available dates. We are deciding between Aug. 19th and 26th of 2016 and have a guest list of 200 people (expected 180).

Any details you can provide would be appreciated! Thanks so much!

Katie

Here is a great technique to combat this issue.

- Change your subject line, so it stands out from the others.
- Keep your emails short.
- End the email with a question. Humans instinctively will answer questions however if you put the question in the first paragraph it will be missed.

**** If a client emails you- email them back, if a client calls, call them back.

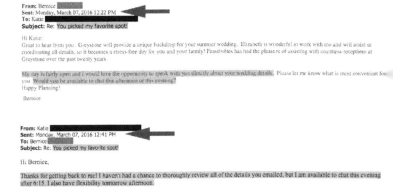

Notice the timestamp of this email it was written 19 minutes after. It worked! Having a conversation is vital.

Here is another example: keep the email short and change your subject line, and you will get a return message.

From: Doug ▮▮▮▮
Sent: Monday, March 07, 2016 3:16 PM
To: Cierra (:▮▮▮▮
Subject: Re: You Picked My Favorite Venue!

Hi Cierra!

Smithville is a great choice – I'd love to hear more about your thoughts for the wedding. Do you have time today for a call, either during the day or early evening?

Thank you,
    Doug

From: Cierra (:▮▮▮▮
Sent: Monday, March 07, 2016 3:18 PM
To: Doug ▮▮▮▮
Subject: Re: You Picked My Favorite Venue!

Early evening works for me, can't wait for you to call !

TECHNIQUE- QUALIFY

Q12 What are 4 ways to qualify a client?

Responses
"Our weddings are typically between 100-120. Are you comfortable with this price range?" "Have you booked your venue yet?" "What are some restaurants you enjoy?" "Have you decided on a catering budget?"
Determine if they will be repeat business Budget- are they hesitant to give you a number? Are they the decision maker?
Budget (if they state from the beginning) What are they looking for Venue
Asking about vacations Employment Looking at pinterest
Budget fits price Response Face to face meetings
ask budget stalk online
1) Budget 2) Educating on the Process and Expectations 3) Venue Selection 4) Style of Service and Guest Count
1- If they start off talking about money then most likely money is going to be an issue. 2- How involved the parents are, if they are involved from the start then we have a better chance. 3- They walk in already envisioning their events with us. 4- They have had our service previously and know how great it is.
1. Venue Selections (this can vary, but it's usually pretty accurate) 2. Asking what's important to them for their event 3. Listening to their language (i.e. do they mention budget frequently) 4. Reception to our menus/proposals
1. Is there a reason for your hesitation. 2. Rapid express refund. 3. When will you be ready to make a decision. 4. Ask for the business
Ask for the budget. Ask the Who, What, When, Where Ask guest count. Make sure to get the budget...(did I say that twice?)
-Be up front about timing and cost considerations -Build the Relationship -Find the decision maker
budget style of food they are asking for the venue
hearing what's important to them hearing their overall budget for the whole event hearing their vision in what they're looking for

I sent 478 event professionals across the country a blind survey with a series of questions.

Question 12: What are 4 ways to qualify a client?

On the diagram above, 10 out of the 14-stated their budget. If we're all asking the same thing, then the client is guarded and expects you to ask the budget question. There are other questions you can ask to determine what the budget is.

There is nothing that irks me more when I see a sales person with an engaged client on the telephone, and they're rushing to hang up. Just going through the motions of their inquiry sheet, asking the 4W's- who- what- where- when and then tell them that you'll send something out and I will follow up in a few days. Having a conversation over the telephone with the client is gold. This is where you can build the relationship, earn the trust and be creative in finding out what your clients' needs are. Get away for asking the 4W's. Think about it, when they're calling you they're also calling three or four of your competitors. Your client is probably experiencing the same type of phone call with all of you.

The conversation may go something like this, hi this is Jane, I'm getting married in June, and then the sales person will say, well congratulations, when in June are you having the wedding? Where is it? How many people? The salesperson may go into a few of what their services are. Ask how they envision their wedding and then request a budget. They will get enough information to send a proposal on the who what where when criteria. Is this person qualified? Do you know what the real needs are?

Ask open-ended questions but make sure you listen to the answers. Too often, we ask a question, and while they are answering, we are busy forming the next question in our minds. You can learn a great deal simply by listening.

What if you did it differently next time? What if you didn't ask the who- what- where- when and you went into more probing interesting questions?

How about:

- From the events that you've been to recently; what are the three things that you loved?
- Now, what are the three things you didn't like?
- Tell me about the proposal?
- How would you like your guest to feel when they leave your event?
- What is your deal breaker?
- Do you have a Pinterest board?
- What is a must-have?

Don't ask:

How do you envision the event? *Every salesperson asks this question, and the client is expecting it.*

BE DIFFERENT!

By asking these open-ended questions, you are revealing what type of client you are talking to and what their needs are, what is important to them. Don't forget; you are selling experiences, you are not selling things!

The questions for a corporate client are a bit different. You need to know who are you talking to. A planner is a planner is a planner is not always the case.

Have you planned this event before?

They will respond with either yes, I planned this many times I could do it in my sleep, or this is what I need…

Or no, I have not planned this event, as a matter of fact this is my first job or first day on the job, and I'm a bit nervous.

For the experienced planner you would ask what role they would like you to take. For the inexperienced planner, you can take her under your wing. You can also let her know that you will not embarrass her in front of her boss. She will be forever indebted to you.

TECHNIQUE- BUDGET

In the survey given to event industry pros, Question #12; What are 4 ways to qualify a client? (page 83) 94% answered, ask for the budget. However, consumers are warned not to give the budget because "the company will use the entire budget." While you are building a relationship, asking the right questions, learning more about the event you are qualifying the client. You have a good grasp of what their needs are, and now you're ready to jump into the proposal or set up a meeting. But wait, you don't even know if this client can afford your company, yet you are going to waste hours to find out? Try this technique, instead of jumping to get a proposal sent or setting up a meeting. Recap with the client on what was discussed regarding the event. Even if you don't have exact particulars, you can give a range price. So what if you ask this simple question?

"From our conversation, it looks like your event will be between $4000-$4500 (or $100-$110 per person) **are you comfortable with that?** Then let the client answer. They usually will answer, does it include…. or yes, that sounds good or they will say, no, that is much more than I anticipated. Then use this next technique.

TECHNIQUE- COST ANALYSIS

When a client states that the price is too high don't just tell them your minimum and then let them go. Do a cost analysis <u>with</u> them.

Here is the script for this technique.

Scenario:

Telephone conversation with a bride and a catering salesperson for a wedding

Salesperson: *are you comfortable with that?*

Client: *no, I'm not. My father gave me $10,000 for my wedding.*

Salesperson: *OK, I'm going to help you with this. Do you have a calculator, pen and a piece of paper handy?*

Client: *yes, right here.*

Salesperson- *I'll help you with doing a cost analysis. But I need you to write the numbers down as I go along.*

(it's important that the client does the work. This is the best way for it to sink in)

Salesperson: *Ready? The venue you chose is $4800. Write $4800. You said you want the look of your wedding to be simple elegance and not over-the-top- that should roughly cost $2500. Write down $2500. You mentioned you want a DJ instead of a band , that should be around $1500. OK write down 1500. Now can you add the numbers and let me know where we are so far?*

Client: *it comes to $8800*

Salesperson: *hmm that only leaves $1200 for catering.*

The client realizes that she needs more money or she needs to alter her wedding details. This is where you can assist her in changing wedding formats.

The client mentioned that her father gave her $10,000. That may seem to be a lot of money for a party for one day. They are just not educated yet, and that is our job to educate them. Often, they come up with a higher budget.

You may be the only company that has offered to help instead of rushing off the phone because they didn't meet company minimums. This bride will never forget how you took the time to explain it to her. Even if she doesn't use your company, she will certainly sing your praises to her friends.

Make sure you meet with the industry pros in your market and get rough pricing from them so you can give educated answers.

TECHNIQUE- CLOSE

Don't begin implementing your ideas for an event without getting the client to sign. If a client has said *'yes'* to working with you, ensure you document the decision. Get a signed Terms and Conditions. Let's assume you are nearing the end of the selling cycle. Your client has the proposal and is satisfied with the price, and certainly likes you. You ask the client for the sale, and they say that they need to think about it a little more. Think about it? What more can you do? At that time, it is important to ask this question exactly, **"what is your hesitation?"** They will indeed answer this question. It could be as simple as they didn't like the floor plan or as complicated as we're just not sure. The floor plan you can easily fix but if your client is "not sure" or needs to think about it more than you did not do a good job in selling. You will need to start from the beginning because somewhere along the way you did not make them feel that they were confident in you or the company. If your client states that they love everything but needs to speak to their father or attend a meeting with another company, that is understandable. However, don't let them go just yet. Offer your client an *Express Refund.* Have them give you a deposit at that time and give them time to talk to their father or attend the other meeting. If at that time they do not want your services you promptly return the deposit. No questions asked.

After you explain the Express Refund, you must leave the room. You need to give the client time to discuss this with one another. Think of it when you buy a car with your spouse. You chat before opening the door to the dealership that you are just looking and not buying today. You like the car, and you're in the salesperson's office going over numbers. Then the salesperson states that he may be able to lower the price a bit, but he needs to talk to the manager. He leaves the room. This gives the couple a chance to agree that it is a good deal. Don't forget the couple agreed that they were just looking, so it is important that they have a conversation to break their deal. That is why car salespeople leave the room. They are not going to talk to the manager-they know the margins exactly.

CHAPTER 10

You Said It Without Saying It

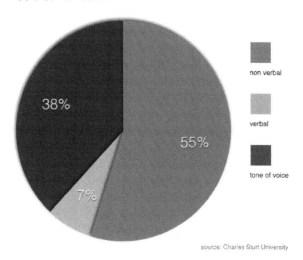

Body Language

55% of All Human Communication is Nonverbal

- 38%
- 55%
- 7%

non verbal

verbal

tone of voice

source: Charles Sturt University

Is what you say actually as important as the way that you say it, and how you carry your body when you do? Studies show that the answer is usually no. Our body language is often far more important than what we say.

Experts estimate that up to 55 percent of all human communication is non-verbal, and further 38% is a tone of voice! After all, as mammals, we have a lot more in common with our primate cousins than we often realize, and like them, we tend to use gestures, posture, facial expressions (and yes, even grunts and huffs) to express exactly what we mean. That leaves only 7 % of what we communicate as directly linked to the specific words that we choose to use.

I am sure you can think of an example of this in your own life – someone saying "have a nice day" in a way that conveys that they actually wish you the very opposite. Or maybe you can recall a time that someone was clearly out of sorts with discomfort as they told you a blatant lie? The Tone of voice, physical expression, and general demeanor – these can all speak volumes, even when their message is unintended by the individual. Most of us are rather good at determining what a communicator *really* means, their words aside.

The main types of Body Language – and what they say about YOU

Whether you intend to communicate certain emotions or not, your posture, gestures and overall body language can tell your audience exactly what you are thinking. Here are the most common examples of body language – and what they convey to the people around you.

- **Crossed arms across the chest**
  If you have heard about one type of body language, it is likely this example – crossing your arms across your chest indicates that you

are being defensive, feeling threatened or are irritated at the other people in your vicinity.

- **Nail biting**
  Have you ever found yourself nibbling at your nails when you are feeling nervous, insecure and/ or stressed out? The people around you will certainly notice that you are engaging in this nervous habit, and they will instantly know about your emotional state.

- **Resting your hand on your cheek**
  Gripping your chin, placing your fingers over your lips or resting your hand on your cheek? You are likely lost in thought or deep in concentration about the situation in question.

- **Tapping or drumming your fingers**
  Tapping or drumming your fingers on an available surface (or fidgeting in another similar way) clearly demonstrates that you are growing bored or impatient. Keep this habit in check if you don't want to offend.

- **Open palms (facing upwards or outwards)**
  When you present your open palms to another person you are demonstrating honesty, sincerity, and submission – you are quite literally showing the other party that you have nothing to hide. This gesture can be used to diffuse a tense situation in a nonverbal way.

- **Nodding your head**
  Subtly nodding your head while another individual speaks clearly demonstrates that you are in agreement with the ideas being conveyed. A smile and a nodding head can start to build excitement and develop your relationship.

- **Picking lint, examining split ends or similar action**
  Picking lint or split ends shows the communicator that you think your micro tasks are more important than what they have to say. If you do not want to let your boredom show through, try to limit these kinds of actions.

- **A lowered head**
  Lowering your head (and therefore limiting eye contact) can indicate that you are hiding something. While this lowered head may be the result of shyness or humility, it can easily come across as shame or secrecy. Try to keep your head level and your gaze steady.

Improving your body language
As you can see from these examples, you could be communicating all kinds of emotions, moods and opinions to the people around you without even realizing it! A quick perusal of the list above demonstrates that subtle movements and nervous tics can be making you appear shifty, dishonest and timid.

If you are about to meet with a client, begin salary negotiations or even go on a first date, you will want to avoid 'negative' body language and work on bolstering the kinds of body language that convey strength, honesty, and character.

DO – practice with a 'power pose'

Harvard professor Amy Cuddy has shown that just 2 minutes of 'power posing' - standing tall, holding your arms out or toward the sky (or even standing in a Superman stance with your hands on your hips) can really increase your self-confidence. This is a great idea to use before you enter into a situation that might make you nervous.

DON'T – gesture above your shoulders

While 'talking with your hands' is a great way to emphasize your message and keep your meeting focused, gesturing *too* wildly will make you look unhinged.

DO – Smile!

Grimacing, frowning and glaring will all send a negative message, but you may not realize that these expressions will also send negative signals to your brain. Tasks will become even more difficult if you have a negative expression on your face, but there is a cure – smile! Forcing yourself to smile can actually help to improve your mood and help you to conquer even your most dreaded tasks with ease! Furthermore, you might need to ask a friend what you're 'resting face' resembles.

DON'T – Fidget

Just like an uncomfortable child, when an adult fidgets while listening, it very clearly sends a message to those around them that they are bored and unprofessional. If you are a constant fidgeter, consider this your number one challenge– spend time practicing standing and sitting still.

Body Language and Sales – Closing the Deal

So, what does the above information mean for individuals in the sales industry who rely on using their body language to close deals? Well, for one – you need to always remember that even if you are not conscious of your body language, your clients certainly are. While your words may convey a spectacular proposal ideally suited to their event, if your body language is communicating worry, doubt and anxiety you are likely going to kill your sale. Be mindful of the dos and don'ts above and radiate confidence, calm and skill – you'll increase your sales and your bottom line.

CHAPTER 11

And The Survey Says....

Did you know that special event companies have similar triumphs & tribulations from all around the country regardless of their shape and size?

Well, it's true! I have the wonderful opportunity to work with caterers from north to south, east to west & everything in between. Large and small, newbies & veterans. A company can't rely solely on word of mouth. The sales department of 1 or 100 has a substantial influence on the profitability of the business. I was curious to know more about the event industry sales departments around the country.

I sent a survey to 478 companies and asked them 10 questions.

Here are the results:

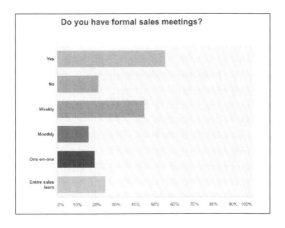

Sales meetings are important to keep a team healthy. This isn't an ops meeting or hash over last weekend's events or go over future events. This should be strictly a sales meeting monitoring sales tracking, opportunities within the team and education. It's best to keep this the same day & time.

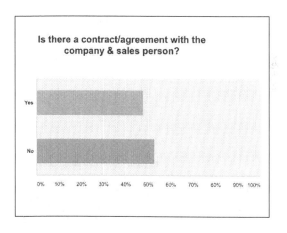

Is there a contract/agreement with the company & sales person?

It's a bit surprising how many companies don't have this in place. A contract/agreement between a sales person and company is prudent and protects both parties. It spells out job description, goals, compensation and benefits.

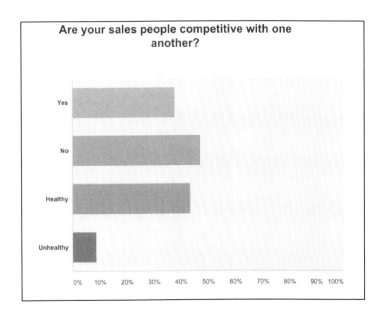

Healthy competition is a great motivator. Display individual sales goals and watch how your sales people celebrate each other. A fun sales contest is always a win-win.

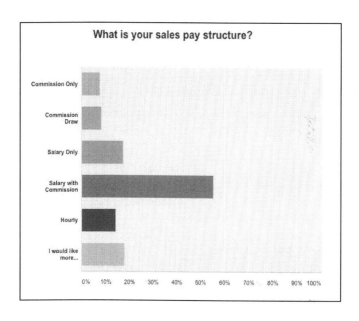

Salary with commission works best for the sales person and company. It makes the sales person a little hungry and releases the pressure of making ends meet in the slower months. One of the most common ways to compute compensation is to add the salary and commission together, and that total should be between 5-9% of their total sales, pre-tax .

This percentage varies around the country.

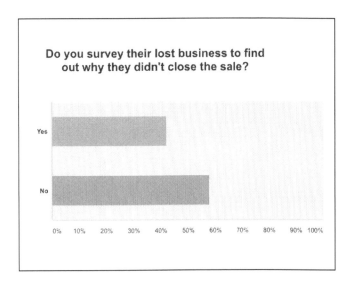

Tracking lost business is a great indicator for a myriad of reasons. If you continually see the same reason it gives you a chance to fix the issue. It could be as simple as that you didn't offer their favorite dessert or as serious as the client didn't like your food. If you don't ask they won't tell.

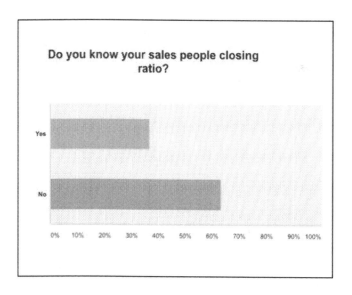

Tracking closing ratio is important for both sales person and management. If it's too low then retraining may be needed. If it's too high then prices may need to be raised. Most companies track using this formula:
Meeting/Proposal ÷ # Booked.

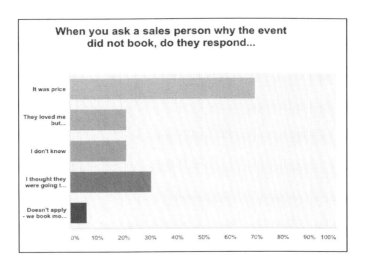

When you ask a sales person why the event did not book, do they respond...

Clients may very well tell the sales person that they didn't get the booking due to price. But the real reason is that they didn't show the client the differences between the two companies. Think about it, if one company is $2000, and the other company was $2400 and the client doesn't see the difference then they will always go with price. Unfortunately, clients still may view caterers as a commodity. It is our job as salespeople to show the clients WHY you're different. Remember features tell-benefits sell.

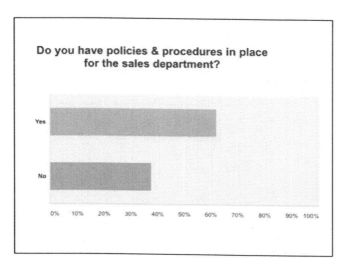

Policies & procedures for the sales department expedite the training process and ALMOST eliminates, "Oh, I didn't know that." However, if they don't read them it negates the entire process. Sales people need to read, sign off and be accountable for all policies & procedures.

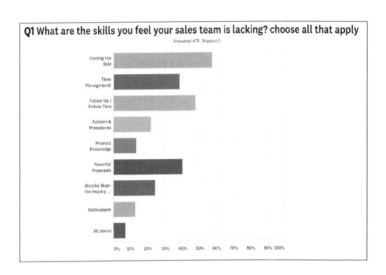

Q1 What are the skills you feel your sales team is lacking? choose all that apply

Answered 478 Skipped 0

- Closing the Sale
- Time Management
- Follow Up / Follow Thru
- Policies & Procedures
- Product Knowledge
- Powerful Proposals
- Step by Step- the Inquiry ...
- Enthusiasm
- All above

0% 10% 20% 30% 40% 50% 60% 70% 80% 90% 100%

I'm not surprised to see that closing the sale is #1. 65% of our salespeople are truly not "salespeople" They enter this industry because they have a passion for events. Most companies don't even call them salespeople in fear that they don't want to be "salesy" They are indeed salespeople which is a different personality type, however, salespeople can be taught the sales process and to ask for the sale.

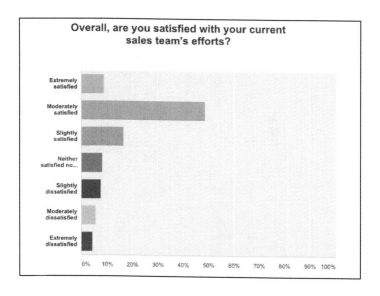

It's refreshing to see that 10% of the companies that were polled are extremely satisfied with their sales team performance and 50% were moderately satisfied. The remaining 40% may need to look at retraining the sales team.

CHAPTER 12

Turning Order Takers into Sales People

Not long ago, I received a call from a rather frustrated caterer. He felt as though his sales people were order takers. I asked him why he felt that way, and his response was that they don't leave their desks to go out and prospect. It was an issue that caused him concern and frustration, but also one I was able to help with.

What is an Order Taker?

Typically, 'order taker' is a derogatory term that is used to describe a person who has a sales job and title, but does not actually sell services/products, etc. However, I have my own definition of an order taker when compared to a sales person.

A customer will decide what they want to purchase, and will then contact the business in question so that they can place their order. What the order taker will do is process the order, and may suggest a few add-on items if they are applicable. However, they mostly cover the four W's: who, what, where, when. Once this has been done, the sale is complete.

If the customer knows what they need, then an order taker is generally all that is required. The main issues with order takers, however, is that they by and large offer commodities. These are, for the most part, identifiable by cost, delivery, and the simplicity of ordering.

Some people think that because their sales people don't actively prospect and instead only handle the phone and email inquiries, they are order takers. However, my definition of the term does not agree with this. They are inside sales people. The moment a sales person begins to interact with a customer (or prospect), the customer is judging them first.

They are judging not only the sales person, but also what they are buying, and then the company. The interaction determines all of this. The customer must feel as though they can trust the sales person, but also like them and believe in what they have to offer.

The Events Industry: What Does It Do?

The events industry is a powerful one. It invokes emotion in people and is, in many ways, an emotional purchase. This relates to events such as weddings, galas, and retirement celebrations. It is also a unique industry, as most people are in the field not because they excel in a certain area, but because they are passionate. They are passionate about cooking, design, planning. They are even passionate about making the client happy. The events industry revolves around passion and the fantastic results that it brings.

We ask our people to do the following:

- Prospect
- Sell
- Book
- Plan
- Execute

These five skill sets need to be mastered by sales people, and our people have to be trained in all five. The thing is, an order taker can be a sales person. It is all about having the right skill set and knowing when to use it.

Making the Change

The next step you need to take is helping your team make the change, turning them into sales people instead of order takers. The process is not always a fast one, and it can take time for your team to full transition. Here are how you can give your team a push in the right direction.

The first thing to do is to make sure that you take things slowly. You need to have realistic expectations of your team and cannot take things too fast. Patience is key when it comes to transitions like this. You may even find yourself needing to bring in a team of professionals to help train them, but the results are often worth the extra effort. 70% of order takers will make a good and smooth transition to sales people given enough time and training.

A salesperson is engaging and hunts for prospects. They develop a relationship with their customer that is built on trust, as well as a pleasant attitude. They have strategies in place for the clients they want to sell to, and often they will sell 6-12 months in advance. They are passionate, skilled, and know what their clients want and need. Plus, they are continually prospecting.

A salesperson spends time planning the future, and they aren't always about closing the deal and moving straight onto the next call. While they do listen to what the customer wants, they also make suggestions and help them to find the best deal and product for their needs. Unlike order takers, they don't rely on low hanging fruit.

How This Helps Your Events Team
Here are some of the ways in which turning your order takers into sales people can help your events team.
It helps them to ask open-ended questions. Order takers aren't really known for their engagement with customers. They usually just process what the client has

asked for. However, sales people are there to build a relationship and make sure the customer has everything they need. Asking open-ended questions allows the customer to fill in any details they may have missed, and creates an opportunity for the sales person to make suggestions.

Sales people are positive and chatty; these are some of the things that define them. A positive attitude and ensuring that they do not argue with their prospects is an easy recipe for success in the sales field. In addition to this, using storytelling can often be advantageous. Putting the product into a scenario that involves the client is a valuable skill for the sales person, as it helps the clients to visualize themselves using the product in that situation.

Turning into a sales person from an order taker also helps them to become more fluid with their conversation with a prospect. Generally, an order taker will use the same script over and over as they go between calls and clients. A sales person is able to bring it up a notch and mix up their questions and responses, creating a unique experience for each client.

The reason these things help the events industry is because the people booking events want to use businesses that employ people who are passionate, eager, and ready to work with them to create the best possible event. Clients want people are friendly and eager to please, but also provide a solid representation of the company that they are working for. The events industry is one that is alive, and the people working for it, especially in the sales sector, need to be just as lively.

To Conclude

Sometimes you need order takers. They come in handy, and their skills can be required. However, it's better to have employees that can be both order takers and sales people. Turning your order takers into sales people can take time, but in the events industry, it is also incredibly beneficial. While it can take some time to achieve, the results are worth it, and you will end up with a fantastic team of passionate and dedicated individuals.

CHAPTER 13

Leveraging Social Media

I know what you're thinking—another article on social media? But read on...there are some things you may not know.

Social media is a viable tool for marketing your products and services, and managing your brand identity. It is inexpensive, easy to work with, and offers a great network of potential clients. Social media is all about conversation and building effective relationships. Facebook, Twitter, Google+, and Instagram (among others) are all avenues to sell your company's products.

Social media is powering the world in ways we could never have imagined years ago. Today, connections are formed out of thin air. Imagine the millions of people that use social networking applications daily. Did you know that 22 percent of Americans use social media multiple times in a single day? Selling your company in today's competitive market involves a savvy use of these resources. There are tons of social media applications and websites available; however, there is also need to choose carefully before investing your time and energy. You should invest in a platform that supports your brand image.

Facebook

Facebook remains the best platform for creating brand awareness—its user base is diverse, and nearly 75 percent of adults use it. Tell me, how then is this not an excellent channel through which you could build your brand and sell it to the world? Setting up a Facebook page isn't enough, however. It needs to be interactive, drive the conversation, and promote your brand all at the same time. If you only promote your products and services, you will lose viewers. Try adding interesting tidbits: for example, a blurb about the history of pasta. To encourage conversation, you could post trivia and questions like, "when you were growing up, what was your favorite comfort food?" How about a category for each day of the week:

Monday – "Foodies, Can You Guess This?"

Tuesday – "What's Happening in the Kitchen Today?"

Wednesday – "Recipe of the Week."

Thursday – "Event of the Week" and so on.

Endeavor to provide your followers with something that piques their interest and that they can also share with other people.

There is also the option of Facebook group or business (fan) pages. Business and fan pages let you measure your traffic. With fan pages, you can add feeds from other applications like YouTube Box, Flicker, and Twitter. For Facebook groups, you don't have that many options. When your fans take action on your page, their actions will be documented on the news feeds of their personal pages. Their friends could see the news feeds and check out your business page. Fan pages stand out on profiles, whereas group pages get lost in the mix. Fan pages enable you to provide unlimited news or updates, while Facebook groups are limited to a definite number.

Instagram

Businesses, especially those that rely heavily on images, have lately have been flocking to Instagram in droves, and rightly so—because Instagram allows you to sell your company by posting images and short videos. While many companies have difficulty getting relevant content, we are very fortunate. Every day there is a new event to capture. I am lucky that my company has a professional photographer at most of our events. Make sure when posting to give the photographer credit.

Pinterest, YouTube

Pinterest is a terrific social network, allowing you to reach people through their specific interests. When setting up your business page, make it easy for visitors and name your boards: Culinary, Design, Cocktails, Weddings, and for each photo make sure you add descriptive words so it can continue to be "re-pinned"—shared, that is. Video sharing services like YouTube allow you to add captivating videos of your products and services. When using YouTube, make sure you properly brand the beginning and end of your video with contact information.

Blogs & email

Blogging is also a wonderful way to sell your brand, as search engines easily pick them up. Start a blog that is attached to your Facebook and website. Platforms such as WordPress and Joomla make it easy to promote yourself to your target audience. On these platforms, you can post about topics that will pique the interest of your audience, and they will find educational, while at the same time highlight your unique skills and experience. Did you know that blog posts with images receive 94 percent more views? Don't be afraid to make use of visual content.

Email marketing is also very beneficial. You can send an email blast teaser to direct people to your Facebook, blog, or website. Another way—add link icons of your blogs, Facebook pages, Instagram, and Twitter accounts to your email signature and all direct Internet mail.

Keep in mind that people who post on your Facebook page, tweet about you, or comment on your blog want to be heard. It is crucial that you engage with your social community and answer or comment promptly. With building your brand on social media, you should be careful who is representing your brand. Your employees play a big part in the brand management and will need to be screened. This is important with all social network sites. Every single piece of content shared should support your brand identity. Poor choices of content and bad images tend to reflect poorly on your company. Set guidelines for your team to follow, suggest different accounts for business and personal, and encourage them to play an active role in the company brand strategy. The old expression, it's not what you know; it's who you know holds true in this new age marketing strategy.

Continue to tweet, blog, and post—and watch your efforts flourish.

CHAPTER 14

Guerilla Marketing

What's the buzz on this hot tactic?

"Guerrilla Marketing is an alternate and eccentric form of advertising that combines the elements of shock, involvement and unconventional wrapped up with a strategic intent" – **Priscilla Dominguez**

As creative mavens of the special events industry, people in our line of work are always looking for new marketing methods that will attract new clientele and help propel our businesses to the next level. Direct marketing, online marketing, traditional advertising...you have probably tried all of these by some means or another—but have you tried guerrilla marketing?

Firms large and small have used this exciting and innovative style of marketing in order to generate excitement and reel in new business.

What is guerrilla marketing?

First coined in 1984, the term 'Guerrilla Marketing' was introduced by Jay Conrad Levinson in the book of the same name. Broadly, the term refers to advertisement strategies that attempt to promote businesses in an innovative way while using only a small budget.

One cannot hear the word "guerrilla" without thinking of warfare, and this form of fighting is indeed the inspiration for the concept. Guerrilla fighters are often civilians, and they are usually dressed in plain clothes and loosely organized into a decentralized structure. They use these non-traditional warfare methods in order to fight against a larger and more organized army. Guerrilla warfare methods refer to a fighting style in which the smaller, less powerful group of soldiers uses irregular tactics, such as ambush, elements of surprise, and sabotage in order to achieve success.

Applying principles of warfare to marketing—*really*?

It's true! Much like guerrilla warfare, successful guerrilla marketing strategies attempt to use the element of surprise in order to shock, delight, and inspire clients and gain their business. This unconventional style is high energy, imaginative, and innovative, utilizing surprise to make a lasting impression and create a ton of buzz on social media. The shock and amazement are intended to affect the customer at a personal level and create a memory and emotional connection to the brand that they will never forget.

Why is this a good strategy for event planning?

At its best, guerrilla marketing attempts to connect with potential clients in an emotional and visceral way. The best events are creative, fun, and have an element of spontaneity—just like guerrilla marketing. This strategy is innovative and fresh, and can be a great way to surge past the (often dull) marketing of your competition.

Tips for a guerrilla marketing campaign that will grab clients' attention

Identify your target audience – Will your guerrilla marketing campaign target potential clients, existing customers, or your suppliers? Is it B2B (business to business) or B2C (business to consumer)? Besides, you should also think carefully about who will be making the ultimate decision (if you are targeting a company or larger firm).

Set a specific objective – for any marketing campaign to be effective, you must set clear objectives. Do you want people to visit your website, book an event, attend a trade show, or simply provide you with their business card? Each one of these objectives will be best served by using different strategies.

Select an appropriate tactic – Once you have identified your target, spend some time thinking about their demographic, age, industry and other factors that might determine the kind of experiential marketing that would best suit their personality.

Be creative – With guerrilla marketing, the sky is the limit. Think about ways that you could set yourself apart from your competition while at the same time staying true to your company and its unique brand. Identify a challenge that your potential clients might be facing, and showcase a creative and efficient solution.

Figure out where (and when) you can reach your target market – It is often more cost effective to launch your guerrilla marketing campaign in a location and at a time when your target audience has already gathered. An event that you host or at a donated gala that we all get roped in would be a good opportunity.

Seek expert advice – Guerrilla marketing is meant to look effortless and spontaneous, but the most effective campaigns have a lot of thought, time, planning, and effort involved.

Make sure your social media is involved – In order to ensure that your campaign has a ton of impact over time and across many demographics, introduce a specific hashtag that will help you compile mentions across different social media platforms.

By trying something new and by coloring outside the lines, you can really impress your clients, earn more business, and increase your bottom line.

CHAPTER 15

Master Networking by Helping Others Thrive

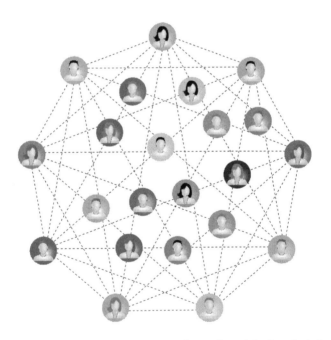

How do businesses thrive? They flourish by helping other businesses bloom and this is best done by mastering networking. As most people are social beings, those who own businesses take advantage of networking ideas to increase and thicken development as an influencer, and they do so with ease. Be that as it may, there is a method to their madness, and if you keep reading, you'll find out their secrets to networking.

Support the network

Almost everything we achieve in life is dependent on another person's growth, and there are significant lessons learned in their failures. Sharing this information with someone else strengthens their role whether it's a business or personal level; relationships are all about networking. The collaborations you made yesterday helped you along the way, and most will continue to support your dream.

You have a dream, right? And that's why it's also important you connect with the right people; to gain their insight and experiences. As you involve yourselves in their world and if they like you, you will come to know them better and at the same time, come to know yourself. Scary, huh? Ironically, it's a dream come true, but first, you must identify your dreams.

Recognize your dreams

If you want to know the truth, people who write down goals achieve them. Those who plan special events know that preparation is critical to success, therefore, they meet goals each time an action is completed to satisfy the client. When you recognize your dream, you begin to put things in motion to achieve the results, milestone after milestone. This is also how we network. By putting all the pieces together, you'll help others, and I'll show you how. Keep reading.

Helping hands

Again, almost everything we do in business or our personal lives, we need the assistance of another person. To plan a wedding, the wedding planner will need several extensions to put together a fabulous walk down the aisle for the bride and groom. The planner will reach out to caterers, florist and other vendors they like for help. In doing so, they help others.

Helping others is yet another way to retain relationships and to network with new businesses. Coming together for a common goal outside of your own is a strategy successful people appreciate. When you add a positive attitude to an environment of helpful individuals, people like you and you earn a reputation for having those traits.

Mentoring

While it's true, no one is perfect; someone will always think you are or at least, aspire to be like you. Mentoring a 'rising star' is a genuine act of respect and a terrific responsibility. Spending time with qualified individuals is one of the best ways to network with other people, and the benefits are mutually agreeable.

"If you want to be successful, find someone who has achieved the results you want and copy what they do, and you'll achieve the same results."

- Tony Robbins

Don't be boring

Once you've recognized your dreams and set your goals, networking is easier if you are interesting to others. Can I be honest? No one likes a boring or cantankerous individual. People enjoy being around other people who make them smile and feel good inside. Others are likely to invite you to network at local gatherings, events, and other social settings when you can engage other people in lively, ear-raising conversation. It's not about selling your business- it's about selling YOU.

If you don't know a good joke, learn one and practice it before re-telling it... please. In addition, a good meme will circulate through social media like a storm and others will want to friend you because of it. Crazy, I know, but it's true. By making people smile, many people will want to befriend you.

A new circle of relationships

The one thing about networking and knowing someone is that they know someone, now, you know 'someone,' and as a result, you all know each other. Consequently, you form an intellectual circle of caring, creative and incredible individuals. Staying close to your business peers is important to connect to other circles... New circles.

Diversifying your network of business relationships

We have business associates that we frequent. however, studies show that more sources come through those who you don't have a frequent connection with. Meeting new people should be a part of your business networking goals. Not only should you meet with these people, but become active if only sporadically. Where to go to meet new people? Keep reading to find out.

Networking hour

Search at least four upcoming events and plan to attend. Where to look for this information? Social media sites like LinkedIn and Facebook provide relevant links to events in your industry as they happen. Facebook groups schedule meetings, webinars, and conferences and list them for interested people to join. Another great idea is to host your own network party! Email your friends and ask them to bring a guest. Make it a big to-do, so they feel special.

Make business associates feel special

Take time out to reach out to people who've helped you along the way. Throw them a small gathering and recognize them individually for the contributions they made to your campaign. It's human nature to want attention and to feel appreciated. By calling attention to your network in a group setting shows that you value their opinions in support of your goals and dreams. Share the excitement and share the connection.

One of the most significant elements of success is dedication. Without that, networking with all the right people, and having them like you, wouldn't mean a thing. You can't treat your business as though it were a hobby… It's not a part-time gig. If you plan to be a top of your game, you will spend days, nights, weekends and holidays perfecting your craft.

You must be persistent, providing you want to move forward. When a plan fails, don't consider yourself a failure. It happens to the best of people. It's how we learn and how we grow in business and personally. Not everyone will be on your side. However, you should not let those people determine your fate. Accept rejections as a part of life and keep it moving; network, network, and network.

CHAPTER 16

Preventing your business from being seen as a commodity – what can you do?

I have been thinking a lot lately about the problem of commodification. In the special events industry, one of the worst things that can happen is that your clients begin to view you as a mere commodity. You know you're more than this—but what can you do to fix the problem?

There are a lot of customers (and yes, even long-time clients) who start to believe that all businesses are alike. They think that we will all deliver the same product. Rather than viewing us as unique event experts with a specialty in our own niche, they believe that we will deliver a uniform experience. As a result, they think that we should all charge the same prices.

Now, you know that your fully bespoke event services are worth more than the competitor down the street, but just try convincing a client of this if they think we are all the same. When they hear that another company is charging less, they might want that price. The solution? You need to show them that you are different and worth every penny you quote them for your services.

What does it mean for your business to be seen as a commodity?

The 'commodification' of businesses usually refers to companies that produce tangible goods on a mass scale. Think of textile manufacturers or electronics components—people have a good idea of what they think these items should cost. The forces of commoditization have dictated prices on certain items.

Luxury goods notwithstanding, if you see a pack of men's 100% cotton t-shirts at one store for $10, and you see a similar package at another store for $20, you are going to feel 'ripped off' by the second price. You are certain to go back to the initial store and purchase the comparable item for half the cost. You might even spread the word to friends and family about the 'poor deal' you saw at the second store.

"Obviously the quality of canapés or wedding planning services cannot be standardized and compared, but certain clients have now been conditioned to believe that they can."

Why is commoditization happening more than ever?

Over prior decades, shopping has become globalized. Intense global markets, competition, outsourcing, and offshoring are all making margins smaller than ever. Even so, brands of all kinds are under pressure to lower their price points. This means that a customer's price sensitivity has increased, making it harder than ever to differentiate brands on the market.

We now know how much we should pay for certain items, and this way of thinking has spread to intangible goods and services. Obviously, the quality of canapés or of wedding planning services cannot be standardized and compared, but certain clients have now been conditioned to believe that they can. They are applying the forces of commoditization to event planning—and we have to nudge them away from doing this.

Showing clients that you are different

So, now that you know about this problem, what can you do to show your clients that you are indeed different than the rest?

As professionals in the event planning industry, it is our job to show our clients that we are different than our competitors. By doing so, we can show them our intrinsic value as experts and leaders in our field. Consumers will pay more for services if they understand these differences.

Here are the three top ways that you can show your clients that you are different than the rest, and why your rates are justified.

- **Innovation is key** – Inform your clients that your services are innovative and that you are better suited to meet their needs than any of the competition. If you can upgrade your packages, 'one up' your competition, and show that you have embraced new technology, you are ahead of the curve.

- **Bundle your services and offer convenience** – People are willing to pay a premium for convenience and peace of mind. Show your clients that your services are more reliable, convenient, and seamless than your competitors. After sales services can also help to do the trick.

- **Segmentation can be your friend** – Are all of your services lumped under one heading and one brand? While a strong brand reputation is nothing to overlook or minimize, it is important to offer your clients distinct areas of expertise that they can buy into and believe in. Focus on giving your clients targeted services under an umbrella of interrelated brands.

Finally, remember to stay away from tired old narratives

While the above points are important to consider and put into action, the most important factor to consider is always your marketing materials: website, brochures, print materials, and social media.

One of the main ways that you can show you are unique is by staying away from tired old tropes. We all need to stay away from phrases like—'our service is outstanding,' 'we are award winning,' 'our product is superb,' etc.—every business says the same old tired things.

In order to show them why you are not just another boring commodity, you need to get to the crux of why you are unique. Try something unique—take risks! Experiment with 'off the wall' ad copy, enticing offers, exciting color schemes, and dynamic social media campaigns.

Remember: never be afraid to be different and make waves, because after all—being different is your biggest weapon against commoditization.

CHAPTER 17

The Vitamin or Painkiller Strategy

When it comes to offering the best customer service possible, what is your strategy? Are you the kind of entrepreneur that offers your clients a regular supply of low stakes services, or are you the hero that sweeps in and saves the day? Do you make people feel content, or do you exceed all of their expectations, blow them away and make their wildest dreams a reality?

I know which one I want to be. Do you?

Think about it this way – if you could only have access to one pill for the rest of your life, would you choose vitamins or painkillers? Sure, it's great to have easy access to vitamins, but a painkiller is an utter necessity. It will help you when things are at their very worst – it can be a literal lifesaver when the chips are down.

When you work in sales, the customer expects you to have vitamins. They expect that you are going to give them the necessary things that they need to keep functioning. But what they really want are the painkillers – the goods and services that will dramatically change the way they live their lives for the better.

Dodge changes the game – Transforming your company from a vitamin to a painkiller

Back in the 1980s, American car giant Dodge made a minor change to their design and rocked the automotive industry. Yes – something as simple (and some would say even as trivial) as a cup holder can transform your business.

See, back in 1984, cars didn't have cup holders. While in car dining was popular, people usually parked their cars and ate their food in the parking lot. That all changed in 1983 when McDonald's opened their first drive thru on infamous Route 66.

The food and drinks were packaged in a way that made eating on the go the obvious choice. Fast food was now sold as a painkiller – something that any 'on the go' family or business professional could simply not do without. The only problem was that while the eating habits of America were changing, the car designs were not yet following suit.

The Dodge design team had a hard time convincing senior execs that the interiors needed to be modified to accommodate drivers eating behind the wheel. They challenged the bigwigs to spend a day in their car, and low and behold – their attitudes soon changed. One sales executive placed a cup of hot coffee between his legs and hit a bump in the road – scalding coffee flew everywhere. He then understood that something had to be done.

The 1984 Dodge Caravan included a cup holder, and the rest is history. It became the best-selling car in America that year, and people actively sought out the model for its convenient cup holder. All of the major car companies soon followed suit, proving that what could have been an ordinary vitamin had quickly become a painkiller. Everyone just had to have it.

Are you already selling a painkiller?

Many of you out there probably sell painkillers instinctively. You are already selling something high quality, important and of immense value. If you're actually selling a painkiller, but you sell it like it's a vitamin, no one will buy it. You need to make sure you explain from the get go why your service is a painkiller. Make it clear that you can offer peace of mind, fantastic service, and real-world solutions. You have to know your audience, determine what is bothering them, and then make sure your product or service addresses this need.

Are you offering something that is nice to have? (A vitamin). Or something that you NEED to have? (A painkiller). Make this clear and shout it from the rooftops – you are a real-life saver, and your clients will benefit from doing business with you vs. your competition.

There is nothing wrong with vitamins – but let's be honest, nothing is exciting or compelling about them either. If you want to stand out from the crowd and be something really special, you need to be a painkiller. Take it from me – it pays off.

Let's take it one step further. Here are two pens that seem to be exactly alike, except one pen is $100, and the other is $1. Naturally, you would take the $1 pen since they seem to be the same.

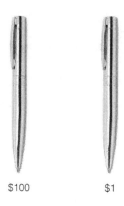

$100 $1

Did I tell you that the $100 pen could write upside down? Would you want the $100 pen or the $1 pen? You probably chose the $1 pen. But what if the $100 pen not only writes upside down but also writes under water- which pen? Still $1 pen? What if the $100 pen retains the ¾ of its value for resale? Still the $1 pen? Ok- what if the $100 pen can get in front of the line for all gas stations, amusement parks, and concerts? Do you still want the $1 pen? Chances are, you would take the $100 pen. Why, because it has value to you. It takes away a pain, a pain of waiting in line. I presented this scenario at a seminar last year and asked an attendee which pen he would buy. He stayed with the $1 pen. He said he didn't mind standing in line. Quickly I asked him, would you want the $100 pen if it could grow your hair (he was bald) he snatched the pen right out of my hand. Everyone has different degrees of pain; it's your job to find out what it is.

1987 comedy-drama Tin Men is a movie with Richard
Dreyfuss and John Mahoney and set in 1963.

The scene starts with two aluminum siding salesmen
posing as *Life* Magazine Photographers setting up
photography equipment on a woman's front yard. The
women confront the men and ask "what are you
doing?" Dreyfus says "I'm sorry to bother you, ma'am,
we are from *Life* Magazine, and we just need to take a
"before" picture of your house, *Life* is doing a story
about the benefits of siding, we'll be out of your way
soon" the woman says "a before picture? *Life*
Magazine is on my front lawn?" Mahoney says, "We
just need a before picture so we can show the other
house looking so much more beautiful with the
aluminum siding" "I don't want to be the "before"
picture - my friends read Life Magazine, I keep it on
my coffee table, oh please, don't let me be the "before"
picture." Says the woman.

The men look at each other and Dreyfuss says, "You want to be the "after" picture? Oh, I don't know if we can make that happen." and she says oh please, can't I be the "after" picture?" Mahoney says "well I don't even know if we can get a salesman so quickly, plus he would need to talk to your husband." and she says "My husband will be home at seven." The next scene is with the husband and wife in their living room with the salesman, he says to the husband, "that will be a total of $3700" The husband looks at his wife, and she says "but honey we're going to be in life magazine."

Did she want aluminum siding? If the two salesmen knocked on her door to sell aluminum siding would she buy it? The answer would probably be no. Why she wanted aluminum siding is because it meant something to her, she did not want to be the "before" picture in Life magazine, her friends read it, and she keeps it on her coffee table which means it was a true benefit. It meant something to her.

SELL EXPERIENCES, NOT THINGS

Most businesses struggle with the dilemma of their company's features and benefits. The sales mantra states that we must sell benefits, not features. Companies speak about Features & Benefits often; however, do you really understand the benefits of your company?

CHAPTER 18

WHY ARE MY COMPETITORS BUSIER THAN I AM?

Perhaps you have found yourself asking that question? Let's think about this for a minute. First time clients who are also using an event planner, photographer or caterer or *(insert what you do here)* for the first time – what in-depth knowledge do they have about your role except that they want to have a special event? In their eyes, a DJ is a DJ, a caterer is a caterer, and all on the same line do the same thing. It is your role as a professional in your line to educate them that we *aren't* all the same. But how? At a conference, a woman approached me and said, "I just don't get it, I know my product and service is much better than my competitor, but I don't even get a chance to bid on these events." Why? Because these new clients don't know anything about you, let alone that you are the better. Keep in mind that people often want to work with people they know. There are trust and confidence factors that can't be ignored. You need to join industry and social organizations in your region, get involved, attend meetings, volunteer on committees. I know it's hard and who has time, but put yourself out there and participate. As a new business owner in the late 80's, I went to my first Business Card Exchange. With a large stack of business cards in hand, I nervously approached a group of people, stuck out my business card and introduced myself.

The **POWER**
of
NETWORKING

It's not **WHAT** you know- It's **WHO** you know

They were polite, introduced themselves and carried on their conversation. I was not part of that conversation and later saw the business cards that I had given them on a table, just discarded. Frustrated, I went to the bar to grab a drink. This nice guy approached me, offered his hand and business card and said, "Hi, I'm John, I'm a DJ" Great. This is exactly how I thought a business card exchange should be. We both observed the group

147

from afar, and I said to John, "They aren't even talking about business." He responded, "No, they never do. It's just one large clique, like in high school." Then it hit me. These people were friends and friends not only like to socialize with each other, but they also like to work with each other. I don't know where John is today. I don't even think he is still in business, but I owe John a big thank you, because that night I finally understood the power of networking. Networking is a great way to build a sustainable business. The benefits cannot be over-emphasized. You get to expand your knowledge, learn from others, get referrals to acquire new clients and tell other people about your company. The saying *'It's not what you know, It's who you know'* is very true in the events business. To be successful in the events industry, you need to have a source of relevant connections. The referrals you get through networking are usually high-quality ones and often times even pre-qualified for you. By networking, you are increasing your visibility and raising your profile. Being around people with similar interests and in the same industry as you, you can readily tap into the expertise of other people with more experience; start relationships that can lead to strategic alliances and joint ventures. You learn about current trends in the industry, this no doubt gives you an edge over your competition. I could go on and on, the benefits of networking are numerous.

CHAPTER 19

EXERCISES

Try this exercise with your team- it's fun & quick.

B. J. Rakow, Ph.D

This is an interesting exercise developed by Dr. BJ Rakow. Applicants were asked to draw a pig. Likewise, please draw a pig. You have one minute to complete it. Draw your pig now. Don't read on until you're done.

Did you draw it toward the top of the paper, toward the middle of the paper or toward the bottom? The answer means something.

Analysis of Drawing

Did you know the pig's placement on the paper has a meaning? Do you want to know what it means to have drawn your pig in the middle of the page or at the top of the page? If you drew the pig at the top, you could be a positive and optimistic person. If it's toward the middle, your personality could be that of a realist. If you drew the pig toward the bottom, you have a tendency to be pessimistic and prone to negative behavior. Which are you?

Here's more. Did you draw it on the left or on the right? If you drew toward the left, you believe in tradition and are friendly. You may also be prone to remembering dates. If it's on the right, you are innovative and active, but maybe you have problems remembering dates. You may also not have a strong sense of family. There is no middle.

Let's move on to the details.

Were there many details or did the pig have few of them? How detailed is your pig? A drawing with details reveals you as most likely analytical. You may also be overly cautious, and you struggle with trust.

With few details, you are likely emotional and able to focus on the larger picture rather than focusing on details. It's possible you are a risk taker and predisposed to recklessness and impulsive decisions.

Did you draw all four legs showing and with a long tail? A person who drew all four legs means they lean towards security and stick to their ideals. Others may describe this person as stubborn.

Who drew a long tail? A long tail shows how intelligent you are; the longer the more intelligent.

I know this sounds silly, but it tells you something about them. If you doubt this, do it with your team just for fun. Watch their reactions to the test and judge the results for yourself.

Exercise

The Six Critical Skills to create a dialogue; understand client needs, priorities, and perspective; and close profitable business.

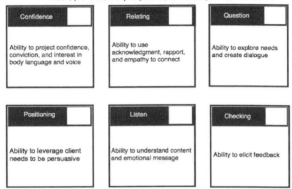

Confidence	Relating	Question
Ability to project confidence, conviction, and interest in body language and voice	Ability to use acknowledgment, rapport, and empathy to connect	Ability to explore needs and create dialogue

Positioning	Listen	Checking
Ability to leverage client needs to be persuasive	Ability to understand content and emotional message	Ability to elicit feedback

Rank yourself on these skills (1 to 6) with 1 being your greatest strength.

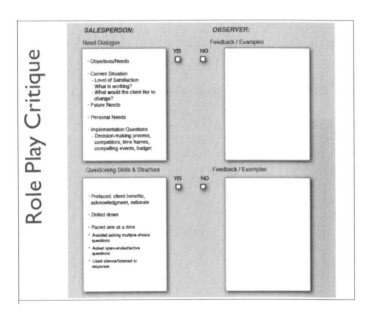

Role Play Critique

SALESPERSON:

OBSERVER:

Need Dialogue

Feedback / Examples

YES NO

- Objectives/Needs

- Current Situation
  - Level of Satisfaction
    What is working?
  - What would the client like to change?
- Future Needs

- Personal Needs

- Implementation Questions
  - Decision-making process, competitors, time frames, compelling events, budget

Questioning Skills & Structure

Feedback / Examples

YES NO

- Prefaced: client benefits, acknowledgment, rationale

- Drilled down

- Paced one at a time

- Avoided asking multiple-choice questions

- Asked open-ended/active questions

- Used silence/listened to response

CHAPTER 20

NOW WHAT?

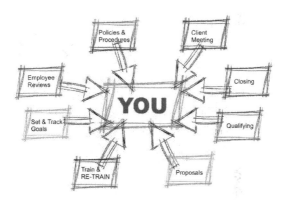

Now that you have completed the book, you realize that there is a lot to do to train motivate and track a sales team. But it can be done, and for a company to achieve their sales goals, it <u>must</u> be done. It may seem to be a daunting task, but I suggest starting with the training manual and then work into your policies and procedures. Training a sales team to sell properly is an ongoing process. As life happens, your sales team will change periodically, and the training starts all over again.

But what if I were to tell you that you can turn your sales team into a high performance sales conversion machine?

What would your life look like if you could consistently hit your sales goals every month- without complicated systems? Everything you need in a time proven and ruthlessly tested format to build a successful sales team is in one system.

Have you tried bringing in expert's, providing books, sales material and spending thousands to send them to conferences but nothing seems to stick?

Do you dread Monday morning sales meetings because of week after week, the performance is either the same as the previous weeks or often declining?

Are sales people making consistent sales and then don't stay very long causing you to take time from your more important work you do to recruit and find new talent, yet it gives you more work to do to get the new sales person up to speed and producing?

As a result

- You're frustrated with the sales team whether it's one or 100 you often think that they could be working hard to close the event
- They do not follow the policies & procedures
- They are spending too much time writing proposals to unqualified prospects.

I do know what it's like, I've been where you are and I want to show you what works for us and our clients I found myself and my employees just going through the motions and forgot why I started in this industry to begin with.

If any of this feels like you none of these things are actually the problems they are the symptoms the real problem? You're stuck in a funnel and haven't yet upgraded it to three necessary principles.

1. **Train**
2. **Test**
3. **Track**

What if your sales people were accountable for reaching their goals and the costly mistakes?

What if you increased your booking ratio?

What if your sales people paid for themselves?

What if you knew exactly how much money is out in proposals?

What if you never have to pay for sales training again your sales team we're bringing in business not just order takers your new hire sales person was trained before their first day you never give a raise to a sales person again?

What if your team didn't waste time on unqualified leads?

What if you never hear again, "They didn't book because our price was too high?"

Finally a proven, **repeatable** sales training system for the special events industry. No more sales books, conferences or training courses.

You're being pulled in many directions. You bring in a sales trainer for the underperforming sales team, and six months later people move on, and you need to train all over again, or you don't do any sales training at all and are very frustrated with your team's results.

What if there was a way to train your sales people to consistently hit or exceed their sales goals every month?

The Triangle Method is a high leverage platform huge results with less effort.

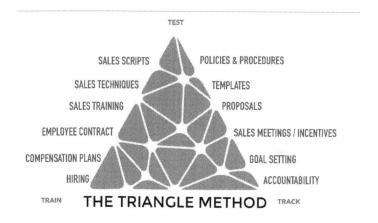

Let's set up some time to talk with you personally and see if we can help. We'll talk about 45 minutes and will map out an exact action plan for you to follow so that you could hit your sales goals this year. This call will probably be the most valuable 45 minutes you spent working on your business this year.

Together we will dial into your sales procedures your compensation plans and get absolute clarity on how to reach your goals as fast as possible, and you'll get an exact strategy to make it all happen.

If you want me to personally work with you to get to your sales goals and if you think it's a good fit. If that's the case I will walk you through what it would look like and take you through an overview of our program that is designed to get your sales team quickly to qualify and close more revenue. We expect new clients to be generating more revenue within 60 days.

For more information:
www.SnowStormSolutions.com\Apply

33318490R00093

Made in the USA
Middletown, DE
14 January 2019